# THE MOTORCYCLE STORY

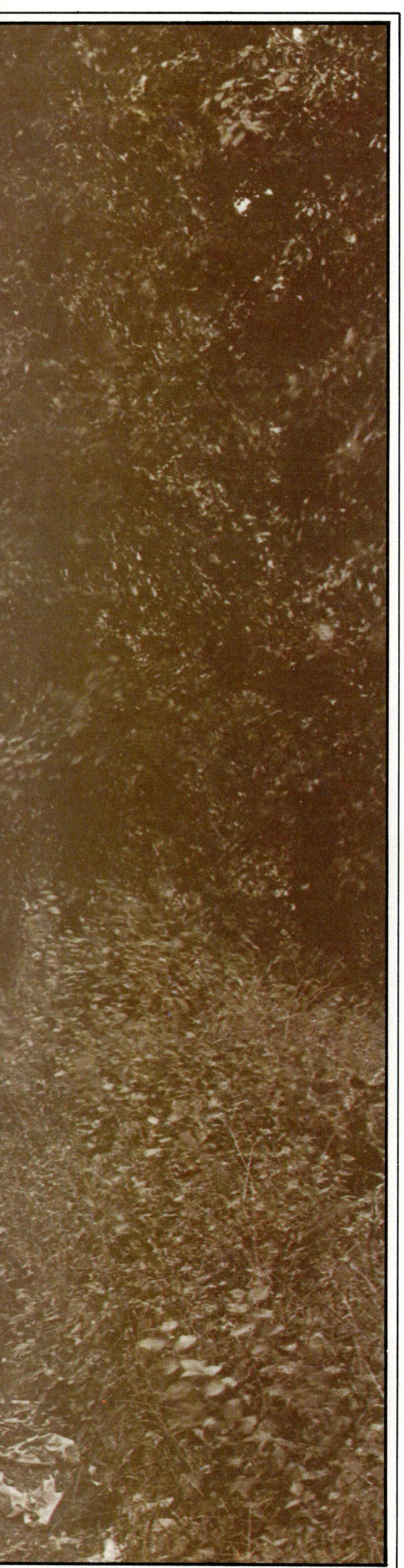

Motor Cycle

# INTRODUCTION

The bicycle had hardly been invented when Man began to dream of saving himself much hard work by replacing the man-powered pedals with an engine. As early as 1869, a Frenchman named Perreaux and an American named Roper, working independently on opposite sides of the Atlantic, tried to create the first motorized bicycle by fitting a light steam-powered unit to a velocipede. Unfortunately, these and other early attempts were doomed to failure. Then in 1885, with the coming of the internal combustion petrol engine, the motorcycle became a reality.

By 1900 the basic design pattern was set, largely due to the De Dion-Bouton 'over the counter' engines and the Werner brothers' mass-production of complete motorcycles. Road racing accelerated the development thereafter and the clutch and gearbox, overhead valve engines, the kick-starter, better brakes and lighting, the foot gearchange – all features taken for granted today – were introduced one after another. In complement came the ultra-economical two-stroke lightweight for getting cheaply to and from work and the exciting multi-cylinder luxury machines. Since then, the process of innovation and refinement has continued and today motorcycles are built in fantastic numbers using space-age technology.

This book traces the development of the motorcycle from the early years of experiment through the years of development to today's superbly sophisticated machines and illustrates this evolution with detailed drawings and photographs. It describes the emergence of Britain as the dominating force in the ever-growing world motorcycle industry and its gradual eclipse by the young and vigorous motorcycle industry of Japan and its European rivals, Italy and Germany. From the early dreamers to the modern innovators, it tells the Motorcycle Story.

---


52 Poland Street, London W1A 2JX

This material first appeared in *First Motorcycles* © 1977 Phoebus Publishing Co./BPC Publishing Ltd. and *Fifty Years of Motorcycles* © 1978 Phoebus Publishing Co./BPC Publishing Ltd.



Made and printed in Great Britain by Redwood Burn Limited

ISBN 0 7026 0028 8

103
N-80
N-80
124
SCOTT TEAM. PRINCE OF WALES. RAMS

# CONTENTS



CYRIL POSTHUMUS entered the field of professional motoring journalism in 1950 when he joined the weekly magazine *Autosport.* He then took on the editorship of *Motoring News* in 1957 and has worked subsequently for various British magazines including *Motor* and *Motor Racing*, and the American magazine *Road and Track*. Currently working as a freelance, he is the author of several books including *World Sports Car Championship, Sir Henry Segrave, Vintage Cars, Land Speed Record, First Cars, Classic and Vintage Cars, Classic Racing Cars* and *The German Grand Prix* (published in English and German). He was also co-author with Denis Jenkinson and Cecil Clutton of *The Racing Car – Development and Design* and with Denis Jenkinson of *Vanwall.*

DAVE RICHMOND started riding motorcycles at an early age on a variety of old 'bangers', some of which now form part of his impressive collection of post-vintage and modern motorcycles. There is no powered two-wheeler that fails to arouse at least a passing interest in him, and his riding experience covers most makes and sizes, from a single-speed Mobylette to a 1977 FLH 1200 Electra Glide. He is currently employed as a professional journalist on *Motor Cycle* for which, among other assignments, he writes the occasional road test, particularly of any Harleys submitted to the journal for testing.

JOHN WOOD was an aircraft designer for a major British aircraft company for 20 years. Today, he and his team of artists have built up a considerable reputation in the field of technical illustration, and have produced more than 100 books which have been sold in many different countries including America, France, Germany, Spain, Italy, Sweden and Japan. The specially commissioned illustrations in this book pay particular attention to the authentic colouring and detail of motorcycles of the period.

# MAKING IT WORK

"Walking is on its last legs."
An American journalist after riding a velocipede. c. 1868

Like the automobile, the motorcycle had to wait for the internal combustion petrol engine to become a practical proposition. Indeed, the stories of both motorized two- and four-wheelers are closely akin, and if the first evolved as a carriage without a horse to pull it, so the motorcycle began as a bicycle without human legs to pedal it. Man being both an ingenious and lazy animal, he doubtless had begun dreaming of some convenient power source to waft him along on his 'hobby horse' or 'boneshaker' soon after these ancestors of the bicycle were invented. Long, muscle-taxing hills gave point to his ambition, and inevitably the first motive power proposed was steam—which had revolutionized human travel early in the nineteenth century.

Cartoonists of the time made much play on the various early British steam carriages, and one in 1818 depicted a two-wheeled velocipede adorned with a large boiler and pursued by three firemen busily tending the fire. This fiery fantasy was labelled *Vélocipédraisiavaporianna* or 'steam-driven velocipede', but over 40 years were to elapse before anything remotely like it was to materialize in the metal. As with the motorcar, history is vague and controversial as to who was truly first to build a powered cycle. No doubt several devices had already been invented on paper, or even tentatively built, but in the actual construction of one which worked, France and the United States seem almost to have dead-heated in the year 1869, with their Michaux-Perreaux and Roper machines respectively.

Both were based on that early type of cycle called a *vélocipède* by its French inventors, but a 'boneshaker' by rueful British riders. It had pedals attached to the front wheels, a 'backbone' frame either of wood or iron tube, and solid, iron-shod unsprung wheels. The Michaux factory in Paris, operated by Pierre Michaux and his sons Henri and Ernest, pioneered quantity production of such machines, and it was into one of their models that engineer L. G. Perreaux fitted a steam engine of his own construction. Michaux *père* helped in creating this *vélo à vapeur*, its compact boiler-cum-heater and small-bore parallel twin-cylinder steam unit being neatly disposed between the 'sprung' seat member and the main 'backbone'. The drive was to the rear wheel by a flat belt and

Smithsonian

Mansell Collection

Steam pioneers: America's Roper (above) and France's Michaux-Perreaux (right) both appeared in 1869; space to carry water limited their range. (Below) This is how a Parisian cartoonist saw the future in 1818 with escaping steam conveniently hiding the 'working parts' of the steam velocipede.

Mansell Collection

Daimler Benz

Science Museum

pulleys, and the front pedals were pessimistically retained.

The fact that the rider's saddle was perched just above the boiler cannot have made for comfort, and although the whole device was most ingeniously engineered it must have been a difficult handful on the rough roads of over 100 years ago, even with the luxury, at that time, of solid rubber tires. Starting from the same basis—a velocipede differing only in being of Hanlon make with a steel-reinforced hickory 'backbone' and solid tires—the American Roper steam cycle was probably better from the weight distribution aspect. Its designer, Sylvester Roper of Roxbury, Massachusetts, placed the charcoal-fired vertical boiler deep between the two wheels, with the two oscillating cylinders of the engine above, bolted each side of the frame, and a chimney passing between, angled towards the rear.

Long steel connecting rods linked the cylinders direct to cranks on the rear wheel spindle, and design finesse was evident in the flexibly-mounted boiler, a water tank combined with the saddle, and the use of the handlebars for control—a forward twist for throttle, a backward twist to work the 'spoon' front brake. Cranks and pedals were removed from the front wheel, making this an entirely mechanically-propelled machine, and Roper claimed that 'it could be driven up any hill and would outclass any horse'. It is perhaps significant, however, that his next steam vehicle had four wheels; packing all the machinery between two wheels was indeed a problem, largely explaining the preference among subsequent designers for tricycles or four-wheelers on which to experiment with motorization.

## Horses first

Having led the world in the development of steam power on rail, road and water, Britain should have been well to the fore in such experiments but for stupid, stifling legislation aimed at mechanical road vehicles. By two Acts of Parliament introduced in 1861 and 1865 steam carriages, 'road locomotives' and other powered vehicles were restricted to speeds of 4mph (6.5km/h) on open roads and 2mph (3km/h) in towns; they were also obliged to have a three-man crew, one of whom walked 60 yards (55 metres) ahead, carrying a red warning flag. An 1878 Amendment removed the need for the red flag, but the man on foot remained, now only 20 yards (18 metres) in front. Moreover, all steam vehicles had to stop on sight of a horse and give it right of way, and were forbidden to emit steam or smoke likely to frighten the animal.

Such a combination of repressive measures daunted all but the most persistent British engineers, among whom two men named Meek and Bateman both contrived to build steam tricycles during this black period. Overseas, further efforts to achieve practical power-cycling proved abortive through lack of a sufficiently small, light and reliable engine, and although hydrogen gas, compressed air, 'weights' and clockwork were all proposed, the eventual answer lay in the four-stroke patents taken out in 1876 by the German Dr Nicolaus Otto.

## Dr Otto's principle

Although originally intended for use in stationary engines burning coal gas, the so-called Otto four-stroke cycle (earlier outlined by a French scientist named Beau de Rochas in 1862) was to prove ideal when far-sighted engineers sought to employ liquid hydrocarbon fuel instead of gas as a motive power. The four piston strokes in the cycle are:

DOWN to suck in air and fuel in gaseous form;
UP to compress the mixture;
DOWN again when the mixture is exploded by a spark or hot tube;
UP to expel the burnt gases.

This remains the basic principle on which the internal combustion petrol (gasoline) engine works to this day. Only the methods of construction, number of cylinders, head design, ignition system, valves and valve gear, crankshaft speed, type of bearings and method of carburation (i.e. vaporization of the petrol) have been changed or refined with time.

Associated with Otto at his Deutz factory, near Cologne, were two brilliant engineers, Gottlieb Daimler and Wilhelm Maybach, and their efforts were largely responsible for the perfection of the four-stroke engine as a stationary unit. But the shrewd Daimler foresaw its immense potential in mobile form, where only benzine, i.e. petrol, need be carried on the vehicle as against boiler fuel and water on the steam-powered machine. Otto disapproved, so in 1882 Daimler and Maybach left to pursue their research in Daimler's garden workshop at Cannstatt, in Swabia. By 1885 they had completed their prototype engine, designed to run at nearly four times accepted crankshaft speeds!

The Daimler engine was a small single-cylinder air-cooled unit of only 264cc, with a suction-operated 'automatic' inlet valve located directly above the mechanically operated exhaust valve. A float-type carburettor invented by Maybach was employed, and the fuel/air mixture was ignited by what was termed a *gluherohezuendung* or 'hot tube', wherein a strip of platinum projected into the combustion chamber, permanently heated externally by a Bunsen burner. The crankshaft carried two flywheels, all totally enclosed in a cast aluminium crankcase, and cooling of the cylinder was by a power-driven fan.

This brilliant little unit, precursor of all modern motorcycle engines, could rotate at well over 600rpm, giving about half a horsepower. It was too small to power a heavy carriage, so Daimler and Maybach, eager to try it out in some kind of vehicle, hastily devised their *Einspur* or 'one-track', as a mobile test-bed prior to building a larger engine for a four-wheeled carriage. For the frame they could well have used light steel tube, or put the job out to a professional cycle maker, but they wished above all to preserve secrecy and so chose instead to make it themselves in the Cannstatt workshop. They cut the frame out of hickory wood, reinforced by steel plates, and the engine was installed vertically within pendant wooden hangers and crosspieces between the wheels, just where it is located today.

The half-horsepower from that historic engine was transmitted to the rear wheel by a belt to which was fitted a jockey pulley. This pulley could be activated to serve as a primitive clutch by being tightened or loosened, working in conjunction with a rear brake through cords on the handlebar, which was twisted to wind them up or back like a cotton reel. The wheels were spoked carriage-type, made of wood, with iron tires, and two tiny sprung outrigger wheels were fitted to help support at low speeds, somewhat contradicting its 'two-wheeler' status.

The men who made motorcycling possible: Nicolaus Otto (far left), whose 4-stroke engine patents made the petrol engine a practical possibility; Gottlieb Daimler (left) whose petrol-burning 'Einspur' was the ancestor of all modern motorcycles; and Wilhelm Maybach (right), Daimler's right-hand man, who helped to perfect his engine. The 'Einspur' (left centre and below) had a 264cc single-cylinder fan-cooled engine.

Daimler Benz

Daimler Benz

Bildarchiv Preussischer Kulturbesitz

Mary Evans

**Steam power still lured inventors like the American Lucius Copeland who motorized this 'penny-farthing' (left) in 1884. Petrol engines were more practical, however, and the German Hildebrand & Wolfmuller was the world's first production motorcycle. It is seen (above) as in the patent and (below) as it appeared, with 1½ litre twin-cylinder 4-stroke engine and direct exposed connecting rod drive. The rubber strap, shown detached, helped the engine on its return stroke.**

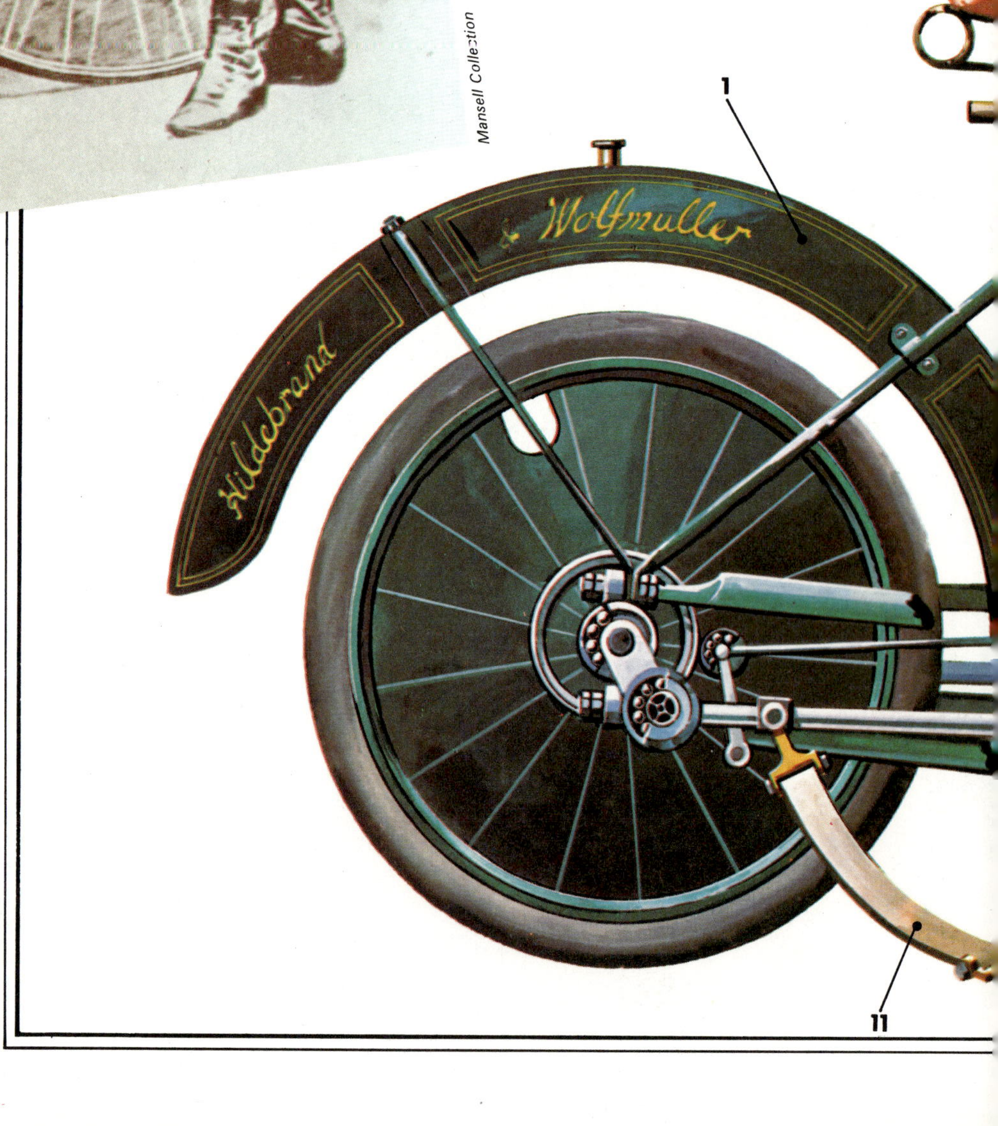

Mansell Collection

Crude and hurriedly built though the *Einspur* undoubtedly was, Daimler's patent specification for it reveals how modern in concept was this father of all petrol-engined motorcycles. Its design features included:

Centrally-located, flexibly-mounted engine
Float-type carburettor
Spring-type steering damper
Equal-sized wheels
Coupled clutch and brake control by early 'twist grip'
Fan air cooling.

During 1885-86 the transmission was modified to accommodate a primitive two-speed device, a countershaft carrying a pinion which engaged with an internally-toothed gear ring on the rear wheel, the rider having to stop to change gear. Handling this machine on nineteenth-century roads around Cannstatt must have been hazardous and uncomfortable. Information on its performance is vague and contradictory, but it is generally accepted that late in 1886 Daimler's 17-year-old son Paul rode the *Einspur* about 12 kilometres (7.5 miles) along the Unterturkheim village road and back—during which run the saddle, in close proximity to the top of the cylinder, is said to have caught fire!

Gottlieb Daimler also proposed fitting a

ski-type runner at the front and a spiked rear wheel for winter use, but such a pioneer 'snowmobile' was never built. The resounding success of Daimler's contemporary and rival, Karl Benz, in getting his petrol-engined horseless carriage to work caused the two engineers at Cannstatt to abandon further experiments with the *Einspur* in order to concentrate on their own four-wheeler with a larger version of the 264cc engine. The world's first motorcycle with internal combustion petrol engine eventually perished in the great fire at the Daimler factory in 1903.

The inventor's reticence about the *Einspur* and its sudden abandonment left the outside world ignorant of its potential. Nine years passed, bringing little more than a further batch of experimental steam cycles. The Philadelphian Lucius Copeland managed in 1884-85 to fit a steam unit into one of the ungainly 'ordinary' or 'penny-farthing' bicycles reversed so that the small wheel was to the front. Two later steam-cycles were the Von Meyenberg of 1893 with backbone frame carrying the water, and the French Dalifol of 1894, with water stored in a semi-circular tank also serving as the rear mudguard.

The next to propose use of petrol (gasoline), or *benzina,* was an Italian professor, Enrico Bernardi. In 1894 he installed a four-stroke one-cylinder engine with mechanical inlet and exhaust valves in an auxiliary trailer called a *carrello*, this being attached by twin stays behind a normal bicycle and literally pushing it along. Nothing came of this bizarre idea, but from Munich that same year there appeared a most important new motorcycle called the Hildebrand & Wolfmuller—it was the first in the world to be produced on a commercial basis.

The two brothers Heinrich and Wilhelm Hildebrand were keen bicyclists whose thoughts dwelt frequently on mechanical power to save their legs. In 1892 they met a fellow *Münchener* named Alois Wolfmuller who, with his friend Geisenhof—an ex-Benz employee—had built a small two-stroke petrol engine. It worked poorly, however, so the four teamed up and produced a new twin-cylinder four-stroke unit which they tried to fit to a safety bicycle in 1893. With a bore and stroke of 90×117mm, giving 1489cc, it proved too powerful for a normal cycle frame and so, early in 1894, their newly formed *Motorfahrrad-Fabrik Hildebrand und Wolfmuller* company designed and built a neat new duplex-tubed open frame.

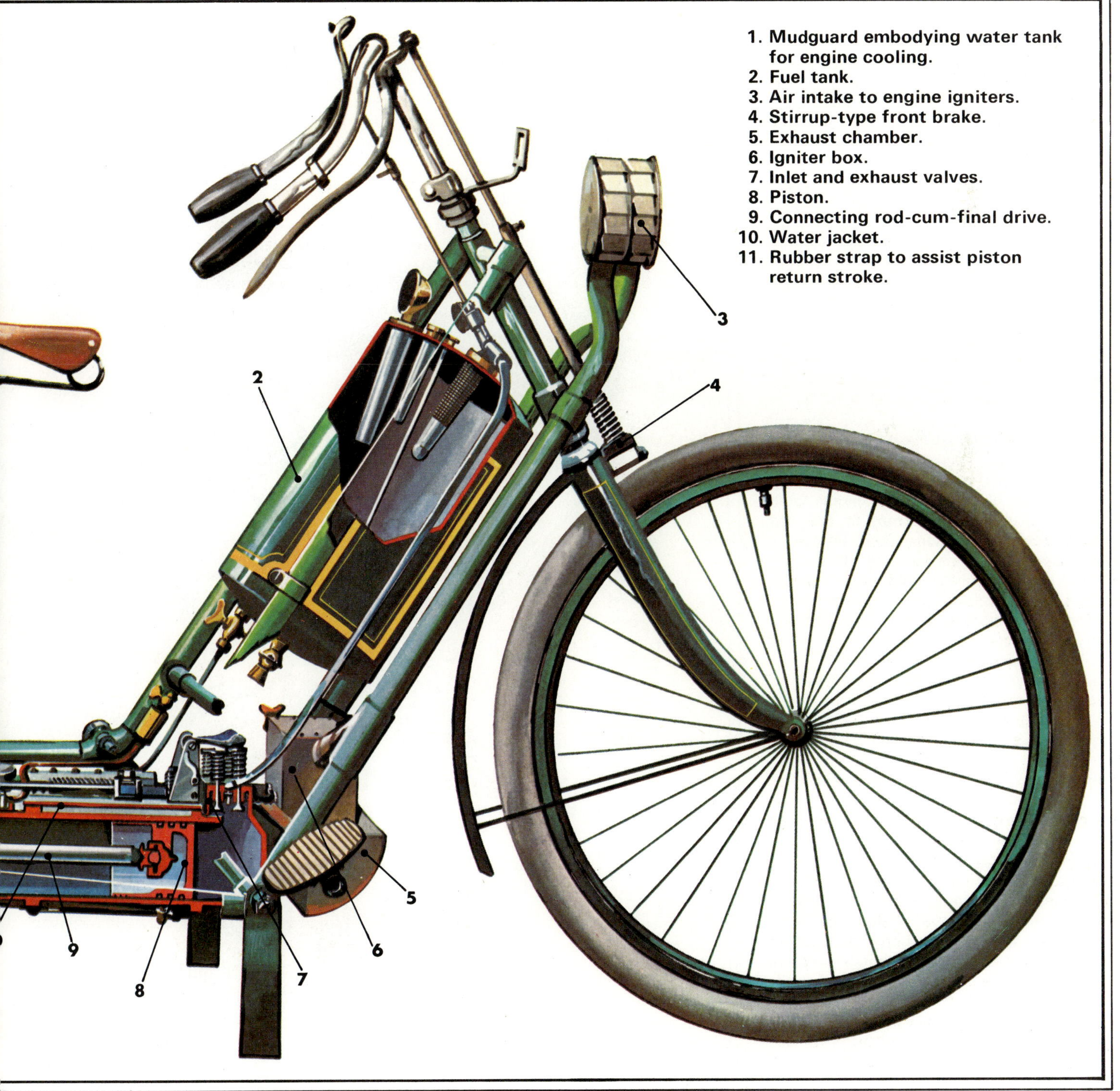


**1. Mudguard embodying water tank for engine cooling.**
**2. Fuel tank.**
**3. Air intake to engine igniters.**
**4. Stirrup-type front brake.**
**5. Exhaust chamber.**
**6. Igniter box.**
**7. Inlet and exhaust valves.**
**8. Piston.**
**9. Connecting rod-cum-final drive.**
**10. Water jacket.**
**11. Rubber strap to assist piston return stroke.**

Mansell Collection

H. & W. They called theirs *La Pétrolette*, and took orders for over 50 machines from French customers in 1895-96. The Munich design also attracted Italian interest, and two machines were sent across the Alps to contest the Turin-Asti-Turin road race on May 28, 1895. The future Italian car builder Giovanni-Battista Ceirano rode one to finish second behind a Daimler car, while Alois Wolfmuller himself rode the other machine into third place.

To survive a 62-mile race over hilly terrain was quite a feat for a gearless, clutchless motorcycle in 1895, but the French *Pétrolette* version was less successful when entered in the more important Paris-Bordeaux-Paris race two weeks later, failing to complete half the distance. By that time it was becoming obvious that the whole Hildebrand & Wolf-

The parallel twin-cylinder engine was installed horizontally, the two pistons being linked by two lengthy connecting rods direct to cranks on the 'live' rear spindle in steam locomotive style. There were no gears or flywheel, the designers relying on the turning rear wheel, in conjunction with broad rubber straps on each side, to return the pistons on compression and keep the engine rotating.

## Into production

H. & W. 'borrowed' Daimler's platinum 'hot tube' ignition and fitted a surface carburettor fed by ducted air which, to quote the patent, 'wafted the benzine fumes' into the intake manifolds. The cylinders were watercooled, the rear mudguard forming a neat water tank *à la* Dalifol steamer. One frame tube served as an oil reservoir, and there was an integral silencer (muffler) in front of the cylinders. Pneumatic tires were specially made by the German Veith company, and braking was by a 'spoon' brake on the front wheel, initially supplemented by a crude hinged steel blade below the engine which was pedal-operated to scrape on the road! The H. & W. was indeed a curious mixture of advanced and primitive ideas, but it was credited with a speed of 28mph (45km/h) and worked just well enough to encourage the partners to plunge into production of their *motorrad* ('motor-cycle') in numerous small workshops around Munich, until a new factory housing 1200 employees had been completed.

Riding this first factory-built motorcycle must have been very tricky for a non-expert. There were no clutch or gears, and only a 'thumbscrew' throttle to control engine speed, while once the hot tubes had been persuaded to function with the aid of a blowlamp, starting was effected by pushing the machine and leaping into the saddle when it fired—the original 'run and jump' method as practised ever since in motorcycle racing. Moreover, speed variations affected the flywheel-action of the rear wheel, producing erratic motion, while braking was decidedly happy-go-lucky.

But the design was improved and further cleaned up, the ground scraper brake being scrapped, and two Paris-based businessmen, the Englishman H. O. Duncan and Louis Suberbie, were sufficiently impressed to take out a licence to build their own version of the

**Strange devices: (Far left) Prof. Bernardi's 1894 'Carrello' trailer-motor for an ordinary bicycle. (Below) The Darracq-built Millet of 1894 with 5-cylinder rotary engine in the rear wheel. Note the prop-stand beneath the starting pedals. (Right) A later engine-within-the-wheel', the fixed Perks & Birch single used on the 1901 Singer.**

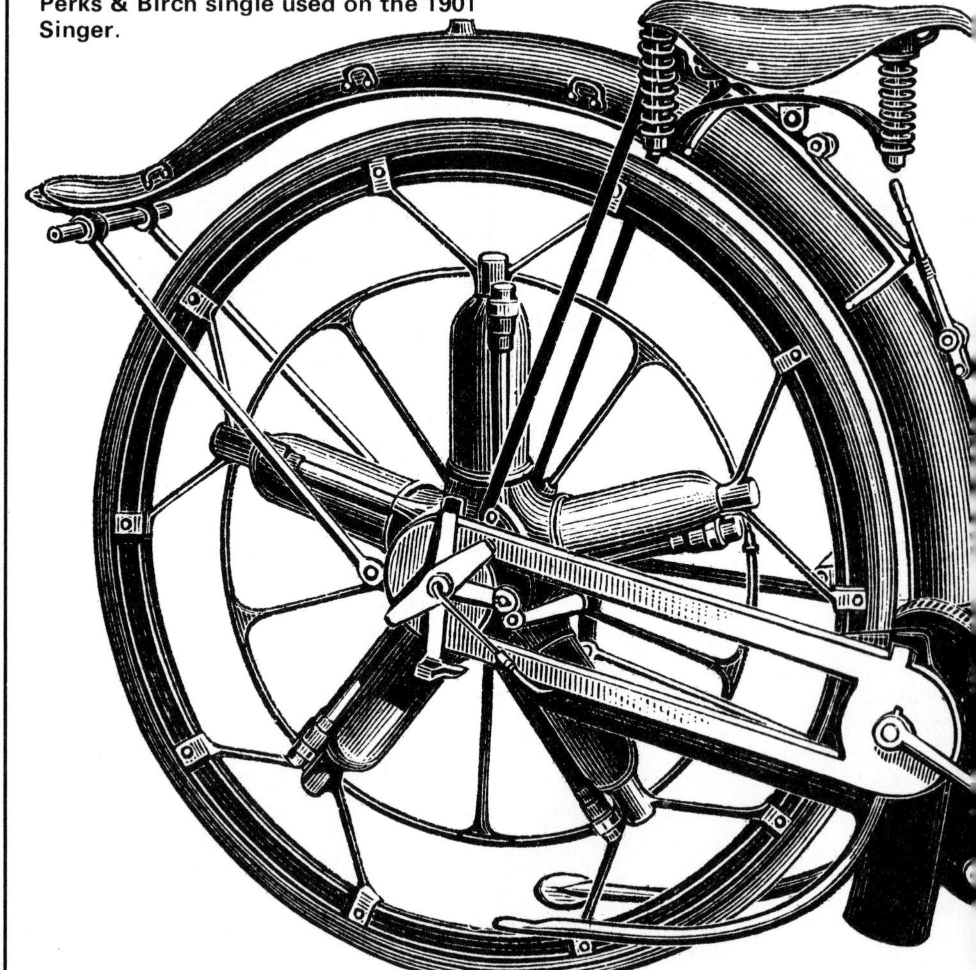

muller project was far too premature.

In private hands the machines were proving unreliable and difficult to handle and maintain. Indignant purchasers demanded free repairs or redress, and with many sales contracted at below cost price the business was running at a heavy loss. It was poor reward for the enterprising partners, and both the parent concern and the Paris licensees ceased manufacture in 1897.

A close contemporary of the ill-fated German pioneer was the French Millet, which outdid the H. & W. in unorthodoxy by having a five-cylinder aircooled rotary engine within the rear wheel. Félix Théodore Millet had actually taken out his first patent for such a unit in 1889, but took until 1892 to make it function. The following year he met the enterprising cycle manufacturer and future motor magnate Alexandre Darracq, who undertook to put the Millet into production at his new Perfecta works at Suresnes, Paris, in 1894. But apart from a fruitless run in the Paris-Bordeaux-Paris race the following year, when the Millet motorcycle retired early, little more was heard of it thereafter, and Darracq turned his attention to building cars.

*National Motor Museum*

Precise mechanical details of Millet's intriguing precursor of the rotary aero-engines, used extensively during the First World War, are vague, but it had cranks and pedals for starting (and to enable the rider to get home when the motor failed), electric ignition, and an elegant fuel tank embodied in the rear mudguard. Five individual pipes took the fuel to the combustion chambers via a hollow crankshaft. The cylinders of the 'stellar' motor also served as wheel spokes, and the Millet had what must have been the world's first central prop stand. The front wheel was attached by horizontal forks and upper spring steel blades, and with the 'fuel mixing chamber' and 'starting gear' chain totally enclosed the whole design looked so neat and simple that it seemed almost too good to be true—as, indeed, time proved that it was.

For industry and ingenuity, poor Millet deserved to succeed. For sheer plausibility and 'bull' the next inventor on the motorcycle stage, Edward Joel Pennington of Chicago, deserved to fail, yet he succeeded in easing £100 000 from foolish British financial pockets. Among the useless patents in the package he sold Harry J. Lawson's Great Horseless Carriage Company was one for a motorcycle. This had its four-stroke two-cylinder engine hung at the extreme rear of the bicycle on frame extensions, driving forward by exposed connecting rods to the rear

*Mary Evans*

wheel spindle. Single and four-cylinder variants could easily be achieved, Pennington claimed, bore and stroke being $2\frac{1}{2} \times 6$in., and able to furnish 'adequate power' with the benefits of a miraculous electric ignition system providing 'a long mingling spark'. No mention was made of carburation, and the inventor said cooling was unnecessary.

Such was the Pennington motorcycle's performance on paper that it was, together with its rider, depicted in an early publicity brochure flying 65 feet (20 metres) over a river after cresting a gradient! One praiseworthy feature was, however, the fitting of large-diameter balloon tires, which would certainly have improved riding comfort on contemporary roads assuming they worked. Although the Pennington marked a peak in ludicrous optimism, this outlook continued to play an important part in early motorcycle development when materials were limited and of poor quality, principles unproven, and designers still groping. So far the Michaux-Perreaux, Roper, Daimler test rig, Bernardi, H. & W. and Millet had made their debut, but none had pointed a clear way ahead. It remained an age of experimenting, and some bizarre designs were yet to appear before the motorcycle pattern was stabilized and a useful measure of reliability achieved.

## Early 'dream' bikes

To two German engineers from Munich, Ludwig Rubb and Christian Haab, should go the triple distinction of building the first motorcycle with shaft final drive, magneto ignition, and an engine forming a stressed member of the frame. The engine itself was unique, having two pistons on a single long connecting rod in one double-length cylinder, divided by a central secondary 'head' with the connecting rod passing through its centre, which acted as a bearing. Fuel was carried in an enlarged top frame tube, passing through the front down tubes and piped to 'vaporizers' in the two 'heads'. The magneto was the first low-tension instrument made by Robert Bosch of Stuttgart, automatic inlet and rod-and-rocker operated exhaust valves were employed, and the front cylinder head was attached by brazed lugs to the steering head in the manner that was later made famous on P. & M. and Panther motorcycles.

The transmission was through small bevel gears, these and the drive shaft being completely enclosed within the lower rear frame tube on the offside. Oil was contained in one

of the down tubes, all of which suggests some tricky brazing and sealant problems, especially in the year 1895! It was indeed a dream motorcycle which must have been very costly to build. It never went into production, which is scarcely surprising since it is doubtful whether it actually worked, but Rubb and Haab built a tandem-seated version in 1899 which probably used components from the earlier machine, but which also vanished into that obscurity to which so many designs ahead of their time are doomed.

So far in this survey single, twin and five cylinder engined motorcycles of startlingly different types have been encountered. The next example of significance had four cylinders and introduced a further innovation in coming from England. The 4mph speed limit and wide anti-motoring bias there largely smothered design enterprise, a major casualty being Edward Butler's 'Petrol-Cycle' tricycle designed in 1884, which was astonishingly advanced in having electric ignition, float-feed carburettor, rotary valves and epicyclic reduction gear, all a year before Gottlieb Daimler's wood-framed test rig was built. Sadly this technical *tour de force* was ahead of its time and petered out.

In 1896, however, the Emancipation Act was passed in Britain, raising the speed limit to 12mph and dispensing with the man walking ahead. Quick to take advantage of the easier conditions was a talented colonel from the Royal Engineers, Henry Capel Lofft Holden, who laid down and actually sold a few examples of what perhaps rates as the world's first 'super-bike' in which specification over-rode the cost factor. His Holden machine was

**Joel Pennington of Chicago schemed out this motorcycle (left) in 1895, selling it, with several other useless inventions, to a British financial group for £100,000. Single, twin or four cylinder engines could be built, he claimed, but rear overhanging weight would have been just one problem. The balloon tyres were a new idea.**

**Robert Bosch (below), the electrician from Stuttgart, who with the English-man F. R. Simms produced the low-tension magneto, first fitted to the Munich-built Rubb & Haab (centre below) in 1895–96. A twin-piston 'compound' engine and shaft final drive featured.**

**Another Munich machine with shaft drive was the 1896 Heigel-Weguelin (bottom), with engine forming part of the frame as on the later British P & M, (J. Phelon and R. Moore, motorcycle engineers).**

*Bildarchiv Preussischer Kulturbesitz*

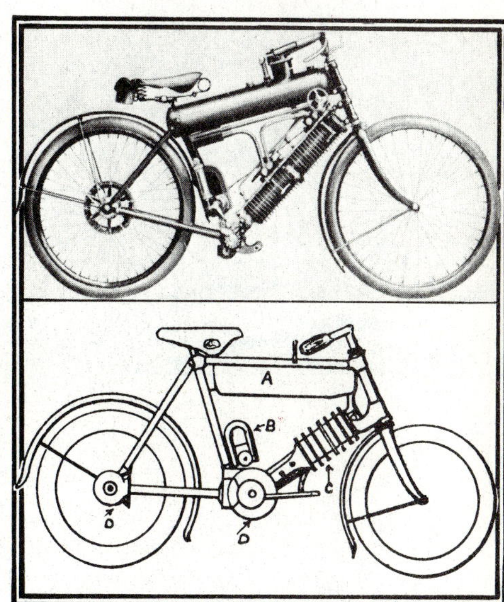

The world's first 'four', the remarkable British Holden, of which several examples were built between 1897 and 1901. External connecting rods drove the rear wheel spindle direct in steam locomotive style. Electric ignition and forced lubrication were advanced features. (Bottom) A 4-cylinder Holden with a trailer chair, the passenger in direct line for dust and exhaust fumes. (Far right): Count Albert de Dion, the Parisian aristocrat who, with engineer Georges Bouton, produced the world's first proprietary 'over the counter' engine.

National Motor Museum

also the first to have four cylinders, although curiously arranged.

The Colonel was clearly inspired by the Hildebrand & Wolfmuller from Germany, for he chose the same intractable direct drive by long exposed connecting rods to the rear wheels. For power to overcome this inherent inflexibility he prescribed a horizontally-opposed 1047cc engine, in which the air-cooled cylinders were in two parallel pairs forming the lower members of the frame. The pistons in each pair of cylinders were in one piece, i.e. with a crown at each end and combustion chambers at opposite ends of the double-length cylinders. Firing was arranged alternately in one cylinder at each end to provide an impulse at each stroke. Stout crosshead pins projected outwards from the centre of each pair of pistons through slots in the cylinders to engage with the connecting rods actuating the rear wheel cranks.

Electric ignition by means of a coil and battery was years ahead of its time, while Colonel Holden made his own sparking plugs from threaded gas piping with porcelain insulators. Automatic inlet valves were employed, but the lack of rotary motion in the

Science Museum

engine necessitated chain drive from the rear wheel to a camshaft to work the exhaust valves; this camshaft also drove the ignition distributor and an oil pump. One exhaust pipe was passed through the fuel tank to assist vaporization in the surface-type carburettor, handlebar throttle control featured, and the whole power unit was neatly enclosed by sheet metal covers.

Overheating problems caused the Colonel to change over to water cooling in 1899, when about 3bhp at 420rpm was realized, giving a speed of about 24mph (38km/h). Although some Crypto cycle parts were adapted for the frame, the Holden motorcycle was difficult to build with late nineteenth-century equipment, and expensive to buy at a time when the automobile was offering reliability and greater comfort at reasonable cost. Very limited production of the remarkable Holden 'four' thus ended in 1901.

As the century drew to its close the experimenters and the theorists had their last fling. A London-built 'one-off' of 1896 called the Herschman had a parallel twin engine, its cylinders one each side of the forward frame down-tube, each head embodying a large

National Motor Museum

'funnel' as a cooling airscoop. The French Garreau of the same year had gear-cum-chain drive; the Bouilly used a jockey pulley of variable diameter in its belt drive, anticipating the more famous Zenith Gradua and Rudge Multi 'infinitely variable' transmissions, while a short-lived German machine, the Heigel & Weguelin, followed the Rubb & Haab example in having shaft drive. None dared dispense with the cycle pedals and chain for starting and getting the weary rider home following mechanical failure. But rationalization of motorcycle design and construction was now on its way, and as in the motor industry, French enterprise introduced it.

## Steam out, petrol in

In the 1880s the Count Albert De Dion outraged his aristocratic family by evincing great interest in steam motor vehicles, and worse, in their vulgar commercialization. Disregarding parental disapproval, he went into partnership with two Paris engineers, Georges Bouton and Trepardoux, in 1882. Their company built several successful steam carriages and quadricycles and, in 1886, a less successful steam-powered tandem tricycle using a British Rudge frame. They then produced a clever and saleable lightweight tricar in 1889, by which time the first Benz and Daimler petrol-engined cars had appeared.

The Count was intrigued by the new if noisy energy, and commissioned experiments in converting one of his tandem compound twin-cylinder steam engines to a two-stroke petrol burner. It did not work well, but comparison of the two systems increased his dissatisfaction with steam; the weight of components, dirt from the boiler, delays in starting, restricted range and need to carry water and boiler fuel all militated against it and favoured the internal combustion petrol engine, which could run for 45 miles (70 kilometres) or more on a few litres of benzine. In 1892 De Dion and Bouton began serious work on a small lightweight petrol engine of their own, to the disgust of sturdy steam adherent Trepardoux, who forthwith resigned.

By chance rather than deliberation, *Ingénieur* Bouton had learned that an engine ran better at high crankshaft speed than slowly, and accordingly he designed the first De Dion-Bouton petrol engine to rotate at an astonishing 1500rpm (the first Daimler unit

managed 750rpm, and the first Benz only 250rpm!). Bouton was himself astonished to find that his new power unit could actually exceed 2000rpm without harm! It had one tiny aircooled cylinder of 50×70mm bore and stroke (about 138cc), and instead of using hot-tube ignition unable to cope with such high crank speeds, the mixture was sparked by battery and high tension coil, with an ingenious 'make-and-break' mechanism foreshadowing modern practice.

Like Daimler's *Einspur* engine of 1885, the crankshaft carried two flywheels, all enclosed in an aluminium crankcase; the inlet valve was automatic—i.e. suction-operated by the movement of the piston—and was inverted over the cam-operated exhaust valve. The head was detachable—and both it and the cylinder were of cast iron with cooling fins, all held together by four long bolts screwing into the crankcase. Simplicity and lightness were the great virtues of this engine, which only put out about ½hp but was remarkably tractable for its time and reasonably reliable.

It was fitted experimentally into a tricycle in 1895, and further developed in the next 18 months. Bouton progressively enlarged it by opening out the bore, first to 58mm, then to 60mm and 62mm, achieving 1¼hp for a weight of under 40lb including the battery and fuel tank. In 1897 De Dion-Bouton put the engine into production, and besides fitting it to their own tricycles they offered it 'over the counter' as a proprietary or 'loose' engine in the jargon of the trade. It proved the answer to many small-scale manufacturers' prayers. To make reliable engines was difficult, requiring special equipment; to buy them and fit them into normal cycle frames was easy; the dream of a 'clip-on' motorized bicycle became fact, and the number of motorcycle marques rose from half a dozen in 1895 to well over 50 by 1900.

Not all manufacturers used De Dion engines, for good things are imitated, and among rival proprietary units of similar design which appeared in the next year or two were Aster (French), Fafnir (German), MMC (British, made under licence), Minerva and Kelecom (Belgian) and Zedel and Motosacoche (Swiss). De Dion-Bouton themselves offered a motorcycle in 1897, but to special order only; the engine was located between the saddle down-tube and the rear wheel in a special frame with twin-tube front forks as used on their tricycle, but few were built, so busy was the company with tricycles and quadricycles, let alone engines for two-, three- and four-wheelers in an ever-widening range of sizes.

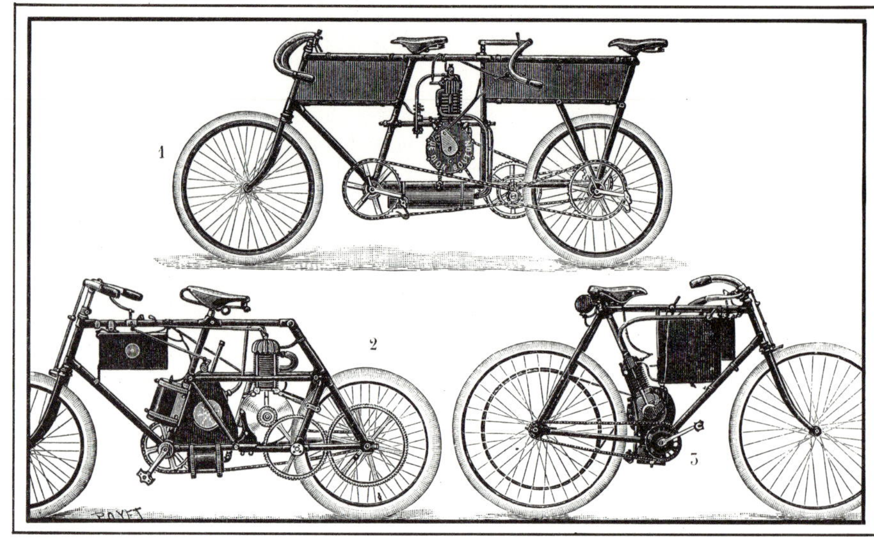


Mary Evans

Mary Evans

**Methods of locating proprietary engines in the cycle frame were many and varied, as seen in the Richard-Choubersky tandem (top) with all-chain drive, the gear-driven Girardot (above, left) the belt-driven Lamaudière et Labre, all of 1899, the very untidy Boyer (right) with all-chain drive, and the Paris-built Werner (below) with engine driving the front wheel, which became the most popular despite doubtful stability.**
**(Far right): The fearsome Couret-Boudin racing tandem with de Dion-Bouton engine.**

LA MOTOCYCLETTE
WERNER
BREVETEE EN TOUS PAYS
est la Seule Bicyclette
à Pétrole pratique.
MÉDAILLE D'OR
ET D'ARGENT
à l'Exposition de 1900. — 30 Premiers et Seconds Prix
OBTENUS DANS TOUTES LES COURSES
3.600 MACHINES VENDUES — Catalogue Franco.
WERNER Frères & Cie, 40, Avenue de la Grande-Armée, Paris.

Mary Evans

While the De Dion-Bouton 'miracle' was still evolving, two Russian-born brothers named Michel and Eugène Werner were busy in another part of Paris, experimenting with motorized bicycles. In spite of their late start they were the first to achieve success. After trying, and abandoning a friction-drive machine, they revised the layout, mounting the engine—a $\frac{3}{4}$hp aircooled four-stroke single designed by Hippolyte Labitte—above the front wheel so that it turned with the forks and drove the wheel via pulleys and a twisted rawhide belt. It was crude, top heavy and hazardous, particularly on wet and greasy town cobbles, while heat from the hot tube ignition burner, oil and exhaust fumes all blew back in the rider's face, yet it contrived to be fairly reliable and a dozen Werners were sold in 1897.

Then Harry J. Lawson, that notorious English adventurer in automotive finance, contributed cash to build a British version, and Werner Frères were able to expand their modest works. The De Dion-engined opposition was mounting in 1898, but by carefully planning their production, the Werners kept prices low and output rose to 300 motorcycles. The following year saw 500 built and sold, while the British licensees also turned out a fair number of their modified version, improved by having electric rather than hot tube ignition. Had De Dion been more interested in building complete motorcycles than in three- and four-wheelers it is doubtful whether the crude and dangerous Werner would have done so well. As it was, by 1900 in an infant industry they had become one of the world's largest producers of motorcycles.

The availability of dependable 'clip-on' or 'bolt-in' engines certainly made the manufacture of motorcycles an international business. British cycle makers in the Midlands turned eagerly to it, Excelsior as early as 1896, while Beeston, Eadie, Swift, Ariel, Rover, Royal Enfield and Singer all came to it via the short tricycle boom. Raleigh joined in with a Werner-like design in 1899, while a machine called the Gazelle was built at Crawley, Sussex, by Ambrose Shaw and his 18-year-old son Sydney around a Belgian Kelecom motor.

A famous London marque, Matchless of Plumstead Road, Woolwich, was founded in 1899 by the Colliers (father and sons) and a Coventry firm, Perks and Birch, produced a remarkable self-contained 'motor wheel' easily fitted into the front or rear forks of a bicycle; it had magneto ignition and was used in Singer two-and three-wheelers.

### Famous names

On the European Continent, the first Dutch, Belgian and Italian motorcycles to go into production—the Eysink, Sarolea and Figini respectively—all appeared in 1898. Another Italian machine was the Carcano, built for the Marchese di Anzano del Parco by Carlo Maserati, eldest of the illustrious brothers who were to become famous in motor racing. On its heels came the first Bianchi, while the first Austro-Hungarian motorcycle, the Laurin-Klement, was built on Werner lines at Mladá-Boleslav, later famous in Czechoslovak territory as the home of Skoda. In 1899, the famous French firm of Peugeot produced the first of many famous two-wheelers to bear their name. The German Star was another Werner-patterned machine, while 1900 brought the better-known Adler from Frankfurt, and two American makes, the Pope-engined Columbia and the Aster-engined Orient.

### A long way to go

From this cosmopolitan boiling pot of mechanical enterprise, no set design pattern yet emerged. Engines were hung in front of the central frame triangle, within it, behind it and under it; some like the Werner drove the front wheel, while others hung above the rear wheel or even stuck out behind it. Transmission for the majority was by simple belts and pulleys, with no clutch to help starting off, nor gears to help on hills. The rider simply charged the grade, hoping to build up sufficient impetus to surmount it, and an essential ingredient on every early motorcycle trip was that strenuous exercise known ironically in Britain as 'l.p.a.' or light pedal assistance. Motorcycling then was a rugged hobby for the mechanically-minded who were young and fit, and still far from being that inexpensive, dependable and comfortable 'go to work' machine it was to become.

Mary Evans

# MAKING IT WORK PROPERLY

"Sideslips and dogs are (metaphorically speaking) the two flies in the honey of motorcycling." *The Car Magazine,* August 1903

The 'motorized bicycle' complex continued to dominate engineers past the dawn of the twentieth century. The heart of a bicycle is the bottom bracket containing the spindle which supports the chain wheel, cranks and pedals. When it came to fixing an early petrol (gasoline) engine into a bike frame, the pedal gear remained very much an essential for starting, helping on hills, and as 'reserve power unit'. Thus the bottom bracket remained sacrosanct, and the average 'motorizer' fitted his engine around it.

Not everyone, however; apart from the previously mentioned German pioneers Rubb & Haab and Heigel-Weguelin, a Birkenhead engineer named George Gibson pushed the pedals farther back and fitted the crankcase of his 1899 $1\frac{3}{4}$-hp engine where the bottom bracket was, making the cylinder share frame support with a short down tube. The Yorkshiremen Joah Phelon and Harry Rayner went further a year later, utilizing the four long holding bolts of the De Dion-type engine for clamping to the steering head through a fixture, and dispensing with the down-tube altogether—a system they patented and retained for over 60 years on subsequent P. & M. and Panther motorcycles.

### Final resting place

It is customary to credit the Werner brothers with pioneering central engine location in 1901, but in fact the one-off shaft-driven Oméga preceded them by two years. In revising their *Motocyclette* the Werners moved the pedal gear back and inserted the 262cc engine where the bottom bracket had been. The front and saddle down-tubes were then bolted to it through lugs cast in the crank case, making it an integral, stressed part of the frame.

From all aspects—mechanical layout, weight distribution, safety and aesthetics—this was the ideal location, as indeed Gottlieb Daimler had shown on his rough-hewn test-rig 16 years earlier! Two parallel top frame tubes were employed, with the petrol tank neatly filling the space between, and the rear brake worked on the belt rim. In this rational and harmonic design lay the basic elements of the future motorcycle. Fortified by some brilliant racing successes in 1902-03 the 'New Werner' layout, as it came to be called, was to influence every subsequent design.

(Left): Colourful publicity at the dawn of the 20th century extolled the delights of the 'new locomotion' by pictures, not words; neither Rochet nor Comiot were prominent or long-lived marques.
(Below): The new Werner introduced in 1901 was an excellent machine which established central location of the engine as standard practice.
(Bottom): After a slow start through restrictive and prejudiced legislation, the British motorcycle industry gathered strength in the new century. This 1902 Matchless was well made and popular in its day.



National Motor Museum

National Motor Museum

National Motor Museum

National Motor Museum

National Motor Museum

Leading makers soon emulated Werner's engine location as closely as the master patents permitted, but as usual it took time for 'the penny to drop' everywhere, and the 'pushbike' with small 'clip-on' motor in all manner of awkward positions persisted for a few years yet. Among several new proprietary engines, the Swiss 215cc four-stroke Motosacoche was marketed from 1901 complete with petrol tank and a subframe for bolting straight into a cycle frame. The Ixion engine from Lille, offered in 1902, was the first two-stroke proprietary unit, followed by the more successful Bichrone, working on the Dugald Clerk system with a separate cylinder pumping the charge. Advantages of the two-stroke included no valves or valve gear, smoother power flow, and cheapness, but its success still lay in the future.

### The pioneer's lot

Although motorcycling was hailed as a new mechanical adventure and a traveller's boon, the lot of the early rider on his intractable single-speed machine was by no means easy. With erratic engine control achieved by juggling the throttle, air and ignition levers on top of the petrol tank, with soggy compression, poor lubricating oils, direct belt drive minus clutch, and dubious carburation and ignition, starting his engine by the 'push and hop on' method or madly pedalling was a lottery. Lucky the man who lived atop a long hill—save for the almost negative stopping power of cycle-type stirrup brakes, and the anxiety of getting home again!

Heavy clothing was essential to protect the motorcyclist against cold, wind, rain or dust, yet the frequent need for 'l.p.a.' (light pedal assistance) to help the faltering little motor would soon have him in a lather of sweat. Narrow, treadless tires that easily sideslipped in the wet, rough, ill-made roads, lack of springing, the slipping belt, the obligation to stop for all horses on the roads, pursuit by hostile dogs, and plenty of dust or mud made every journey an expedition and a physical challenge. Considering the conditions, it says much for man's enthusiasm and tenacity that motorcycling thrived.

Yet thrive it did, and wide public interest in the 'new locomotion' on two, three and four wheels was a great stimulant to the world's manufacturing countries, and saw the founding of many famous makes of motorcycle. A large proportion of them came from cycle factories. The German NSU concern of Neckarsulm on the river Neckar had turned out elegant 'penny-farthings' since 1886, switching to safety bicycles which they continued to build right up to 1960. In 1900 they attached a Swiss-built Zedel engine (the initials of its makers Zurcher and Luthi) to one of their NSU cycles, selling a hundred in the first year, and many more before turning to larger motorcycles.

Belgium's 'Woolwich arsenal', the Fabrique Nationale des Armes de Guerre at Herstal in Liège, had made bicycles since 1898, and in 1901 they, too, equipped one with a small 133cc engine. It was simple, reliable and popular, and the first year's output was 300. Then they enlarged the engine, first to 188cc and then to 300cc by 1904, by which time sophistication had set in and the FN had magneto ignition, mechanical oil pump and sprung front forks. In 1901 also, over in the United States the maker of the Indian bicycle, George Hendee of Springfield, Mass., decided to motorize one. The motor, designed by Oscar Hedstrom, took the place of the saddle down-tube, inclined rearward, and the machine was novel in having chain drive. It ran well, Hendee chased up some capital and went into business. His 1901 output was three machines, by 1902 it was 142, and 546

L. Shelley

by 1904, by which time the Indian 'moto-cycle' as they called it was growing up with the industry and destined for a great future as a 'big twin'.

### Birth of the Norton

The British Norton, product of a small Birmingham works producing chains and other cycle parts, began in much the same way. Their first power-bike appeared in 1902 with a French 143cc Clément four-stroke engine driving a long belt direct to the rear wheel. Its builder, James L. ('Pa') Norton, called it the *Energette*, and supplied it to order only. Soon he refined the design, fitting a primary chain, countershaft and shorter belt, and his next step was to fit more powerful engines such as the Swiss Moto-Rêve and French Peugeot vee-twins, setting the Norton marque well on the road to fame.

The Birmingham-built Quadrant and Coventry-built Riley (another cycle firm) also appeared in 1901, with Continental motors bought 'over the counter'. Another Midlands cycle maker, Wearwell, introduced a motor-cycle that year with a new British engine, the Stevens—first product of the Stevens brothers later to earn fame for their AJS motorcycles. At Dijon one of France's best quality makes, the Terrot, was born, while in Italy Prinetti e Stucchi, whose power-tricycles had been developed to a high pitch and raced before 1900 by a talented young man named Ettore Bugatti, made their first two-wheeler. Bugatti by then had left to make his mark in the car world, and when Prinetti also left, Stucchi continued alone, his sturdy machine selling briskly up to the First World War.

The year 1902 brought a fresh crop of contenders in an ever-widening market. With the

**The British Norton motorcycle, which began in 1902 as a motorized bicycle with Clément engine (top) came into prominence when H.R. Fowler on this standard twin-cylinder Peugeot-engined machine (above) won the multi-cylinder class in the first Isle of Man TT race in 1907, averaging 36.22mph with a fastest lap at 42.91mph.**
**(Far left): A stalwart of the German industry since the early 1900s, NSU of Neckarsulm built up their reputation with sturdy, reliable machines such as this 1906 3hp model.**
**(Bottom left): 1901 brought the first Indian, one of America's most famous makes. Its engine also served as the saddle down-tube at risk of overheating the driver's legs.**

National Motor Museum

National Motor Museum

National Motor Museum

waning of the tricycle and quadricycle craze, Ariel of Birmingham made a neat, simple two-wheeler which was ancestor to an illustrious line. In Oxford a young cycle maker named William R. Morris adapted De Dion-Bouton engines to his 'pushbike' and sold an encouraging number in his first year. Then he changed over to the MMC, a British-built De Dion, and in 1904 decided to exhibit a Morris motorcycle at the Agricultural Hall Show in Islington, London.

## Morris marque

The story has it that Morris slaved for four days and nights preparing the machine, and after getting it on to its stand at the Exhibition he left for his hotel, only to fall asleep exhausted in the Underground railway, completing several rounds of the Inner Circle before somebody woke him up. Morris made motorcycles in relatively small numbers until 1910, when his interest had already turned to the cars that were to make him a millionaire.

Also destined for more fame on four wheels than two was the Lagonda. This was founded in Staines, Middx, by a mechanically-minded American opera singer named Wilbur Gunn, who came from Springfield, Ohio, to settle in Britain. He built his first tricycle in 1898 in the greenhouse adjoining his house, calling it the Lagonda after the Indian name of a creek near his old home town. The name was then applied in 1902 to his first two-wheeler, which followed fashion in having a De Dion-like engine turning the rear wheel direct through a belt. Gunn went racing with it, but preoccupation with a new tricar meant that not many Lagonda motorbikes were built, and by 1906 the Staines marque was fully embroiled with cars.

Rover of Britain and Opel of Germany were other early motorcycle makes that gained greater renown with cars. Both had years of cycle-making experience behind them, and both used proprietary engines in beefed-up cycle frames. Scotland joined in with a well-made machine called the Victoria, hailing from a factory in Dennistoun, Glasgow, while French newcomers destined for great racing fame were Alcyon and Griffon. America contributed the Merkel and the Holley, both of which followed the trend of the Indian design by inclining their engines rearward under the saddle.

## The Holley

On the Holley the single-cylinder unit was ingeniously set to the right so that the crankshaft passed through the bottom bracket, with the flywheel on the left, while final drive was by chain. The prototype gained early prominence with a win in the 1901 Boston to New York road race, probably the first held for motorcycles in the United States. The designer/rider was George M. Holley, later famous as a carburettor manufacturer, who recalled "That was quite a race; cobblestones, mud, sand, chickens and people, but the engine kept purring and I arrived right on schedule. Of course with the layer of mud and dust on my face even my own mother wouldn't have recognized me."

William R. Morris (left) of Oxford built cycles and motorcycles before making his fortune with cars. The Morris motorcycle (left lower) had an unsightly looped down-tube to accommodate the MMC engine.
(Far left): Another prominent English make was the Birmingham-built Ariel; this 1903 model had its White & Poppe engine fitted in the 'New Werner' position.
(Below): Better known as car manufacturers, Opel of Germany, also built motorcycles. This 1905 3$\frac{3}{4}$hp model had a Fafnir side-valve engine, Bosch magneto ignition and a very 'sit up and beg' seating position.

One of Britain's most famous makes, with a history of over 70 years, Triumph of Coventry were founded in 1903, when this 2hp JAP-engined model was marketed. Triumph soon began to make their own engines, establishing a great reputation for dependability.

National Motor Museum

Over 80 new makes from seven different countries—Britain, France, Germany, Austro-Hungary, Italy, Sweden and the United States—made 1903 a boom year for the growing motorcycle industry, outstanding among them being Triumph, Harley-Davidson and Husqvarna. Triumph of Coventry was founded by two of the many German engineers who settled in Britain late in the nineteenth century for the better opportunities afforded them at that time. Maurice Schulte and Siegfried Bettmann first built bicycles, then in 1903 successfully attached a Belgian 2-hp Minerva engine to one of their sturdier frames. They put it into production, first using proprietary engines and then making their own, and by maintaining high quality and good market sense the firm never looked back.

The big American Harley-Davidson twin of tradition sprang from a smaller, humbler machine in 1903, when William S. Harley and Arthur Davidson, both from Britain, built a sturdier-than-usual motorized bicycle with its engine in a loop frame. Davidson's brothers Walter and William joined the venture, and the newly formed company flourished. Road conditions and design limitations quickly taught them that more power and greater cycle strength were essential to success, and the Harley-Davidson soon assumed its massive characteristic build.

## Coming of age

Husqvarna is a market town in Sweden, and the name was adopted by a firm of bicycle makers which followed the European trend by modifying one of their stronger products to take a Belgian $1\frac{1}{4}$-hp FN engine. The down-tube from the steering head to the bottom bracket was bifurcated to pass each side of the engine, with separate brackets and stays to support it. To combat hard frosts most Swedish roads were left unmetalled, thus demanding extra stamina, and the Husqvarna proved an extremely tough machine which launched its makers on a successful business.

Under the new Motor Car Act, introduced in Britain during 1903, registration of all motor vehicles became obligatory. The 12 months after it came into force established that no fewer than 22126 motorcycles were operating in the United Kingdom, and indicated that by 1904 motorcycle manufacture was no longer 'a dabble on the side' by cycle makers but serious business. The motorbike was growing up; engine size and power had risen, with more robust frames, stronger wheels and larger pneumatic tires as inevitable corollaries. Many makers now produced their own engines, and some took the expedient of 'doubling up' with twin cylinders on one crankcase. Set lengthwise in a 60° vee, such engines fitted very conveniently into the triangular frame structure, and provided more frequent and hence smoother power impulses.

Improved metallurgy provided more durable valves, piston rings and bearings, while the old suction-operated automatic inlet valve was gradually abandoned and replaced by positive mechanical operation, as popularized on the Mercedes car in 1901. Magneto ignition became the rule rather than the exception, Simms-Bosch introducing a high-tension system in 1903, and the surface carburettor slowly gave way to the spray type.

### Improving the transmission

Transmission received more attention too. Although the vee-belt had many years ahead of it yet, a few makers, notably Humber, preferred chain drive, which did not slip in wet weather nor in an excess of oil, but was not shock-damping like rubber-cum-canvas belting, and of course cost more. The same applied to a clutch, with added snags of bulk, weight and complication. Some belt-drive single-speed systems were fitted with a crude disc-type clutch between the rear hub and a separately-spoked belt rim—better than nothing although tricky in take-off owing to the high single gear ratio.

In 1905 Phelon & Moore, successors to Phelon & Rayner and makers of the P. & M. motorcycle, introduced a two-speed device comprising two primary chains with clutched sprockets of different diameters on a cam-mounted countershaft. Final drive was by single chain, and though the running was rougher than a belt, the P. & M. came from Yorkshire, where hills abounded and two speeds were appreciated. Royal Enfield lost little time in employing it too, under licence. Going for a simpler system, NSU of Germany mounted an epicyclic two-speed gear on the end of the engine pulley, while several makers persisted with a cycle-type three-speed epicyclic rear hub with internal clutch. This suffered greatly from the harsh, erratic thrusts of a single-cylinder engine.

Another device widely used was an engine pulley of variable diameter, with lever control. A prophetic French machine called the *Magali* had a gear-driven countershaft carrying the engine flywheel and a rudimentary clutch, with chain final drive. It won a number of French speed events but never went into production. Indeed, a kind of inertia seemed to grip manufacturers, who were reluctant to risk a market they knew with innovative designs. Militating against all gear systems then were three vital factors: weight, cost and reliability; the motorbike's chief advantages over the car were lightness and cheapness, and a separate clutch and gearbox menaced both.

### Faster and safer

But there was fruitful design enterprise in other directions. Important new initials in the proprietary engine trade were JAP, denoting J. A. Prestwich of Tottenham, London, who by 1904 were building both engines and complete motorcycles. The latter were well made and enjoyed some racing success, but lasted only four years, by which time the JAP range of single and vee-twin engines, some with pushrod overhead valves, were all that the factory could comfortably produce.

In France the Werner brothers devised a rocking-lever footchange for a two-speed transmission they used in racing, while Truffault marketed some excellent leading-link sprung front forks. In Britain the encased flexible cable invented by Frank Bowden

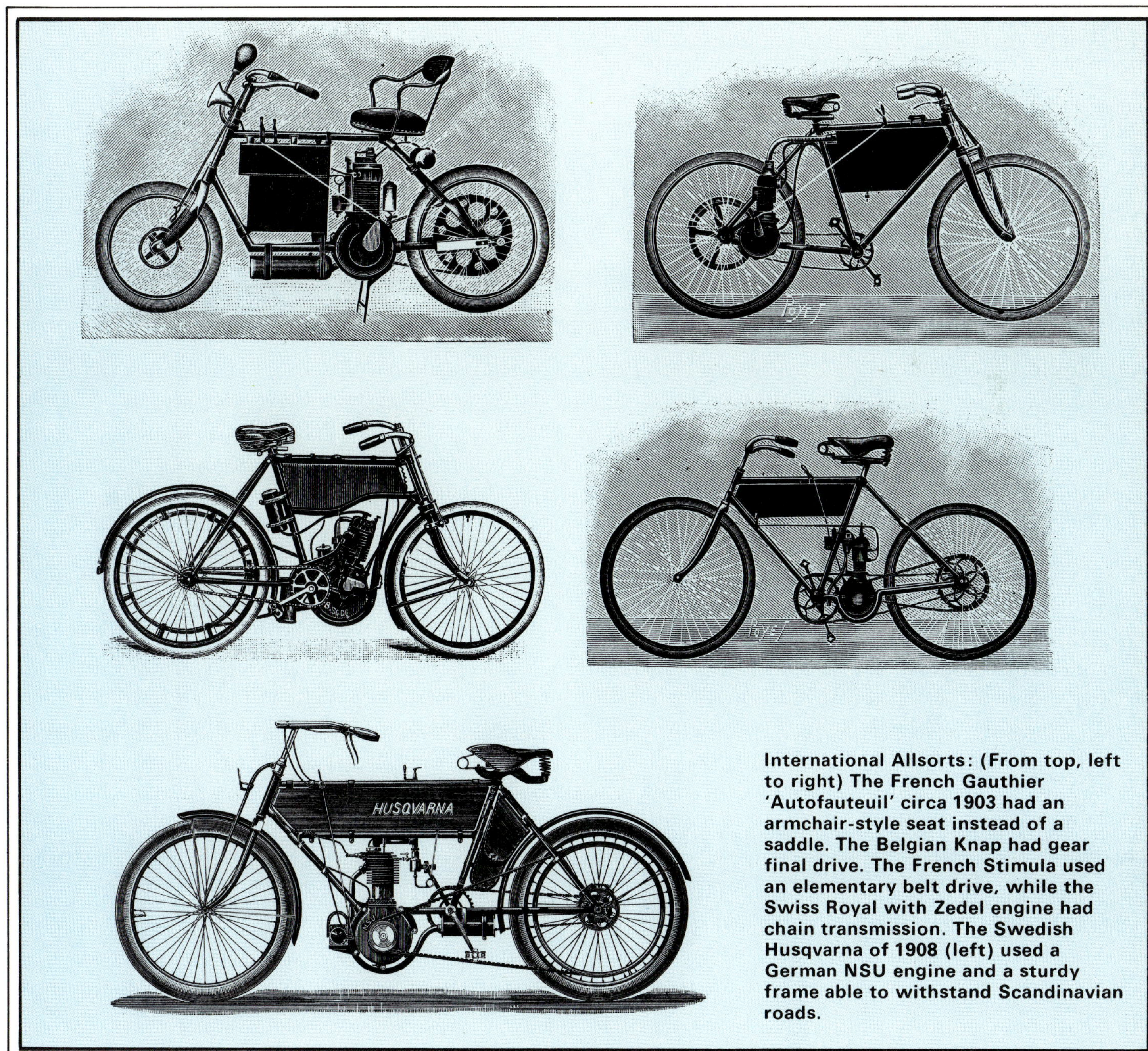


**International Allsorts: (From top, left to right) The French Gauthier 'Autofauteuil' circa 1903 had an armchair-style seat instead of a saddle. The Belgian Knap had gear final drive. The French Stimula used an elementary belt drive, while the Swiss Royal with Zedel engine had chain transmission. The Swedish Husqvarna of 1908 (left) used a German NSU engine and a sturdy frame able to withstand Scandinavian roads.**

Mary Evans

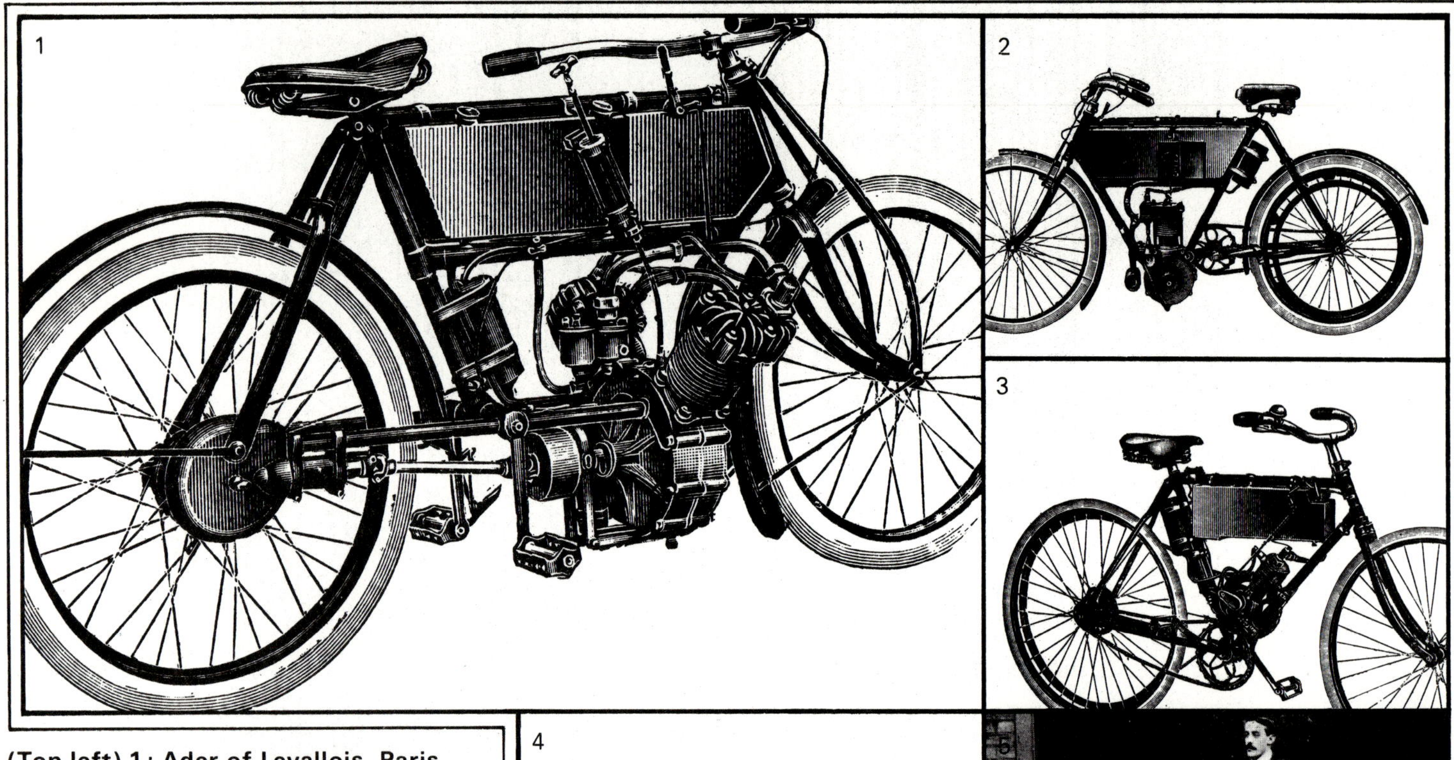

30 (Top left) 1: Ader of Levallois, Paris, built this advanced transverse vee-twin with shaft drive in 1903. 2: The 1902 $1\frac{1}{4}$hp Garreau, with engine in the 'New Werner' position. 3: The Swiss $1\frac{1}{2}$hp Motosacoche, one of the first successful 'clip-on' units adaptable to an ordinary bicycle. 4: The British-built Bowden with chain drive. 5: Another British-built machine, the 1904 $3\frac{1}{2}$hp Ormonde, was a good hill-climber.

*L. Shelley and Mary Evans*

*Motor Cycle*

made riding a motorcycle safer by placing more controls on the handlebars. The twist grip, first used by Roper and Daimler for braking, and in the motorized bicycle phase to cut out the ignition, was more widely employed, while Triumph introduced footrests separate from the pedalling gear, and a nearside pedal to the rear brakes.

Having got the motorcycle to work reasonably well, it was natural that man should wish to have his wife or children as passengers. Tricycles and quadricycles occupied an uneasy 'no man's land' between the motorbike and the car, took almost as much room as the latter, yet were scarcely as comfortable. What was needed by the many who had to watch costs was a carriage that could be attached to an ordinary motorcycle and removed at will.

The trailer chair was an abomination, the unfortunate occupant receiving everything in his or her face—exhaust, blobs of oil, dust and mud. By 1902, however, trailer makers Mills & Fullford built a detachable one-wheeled side chassis, carrying a splendid example of rococo wickerwork which seated the passenger in lofty elegance and a fair flow of clean air. The wheel trailed on a pivot like a castor, and the whole thing could be bolted to the frame by clamps in about five minutes.

The castor idea did not last, but the rigid-wheeled sidecar outfit, or 'combination', gradually caught on despite the inevitable eccentric variations on the main theme to sidetrack development. They included the sidecar wheel turning with the parent machine's steering, paired small wheels, and a banking chassis, but the basic combination has lasted to this day.

In 1905 the Belgian FN concern, having thoroughly learned the rudiments of power-bike practice while concurrently building small two-cylinder cars, surprised the two-wheeler world with an exquisite little 363cc aircooled in-line four-cylinder design. Its tiny separate cylinders measured only 45×55mm, and designer Paul Kelecom capped all by fitting fully enclosed shaft drive passing through the offside frame member to the rear wheel, an internal expanding rear brake, and leading link telescopically sprung front forks. The cylinders, perhaps, were *too* small, but this was the precursor of a design destined to grow into a 748cc three-speed 'superbike' which remained in production into the 1920s.

Nor was the FN the only 'four'. Britisher Charles Binks of Nottingham, later a successful carburettor maker, built a 5hp four-cylinder prototype in 1903—a most versatile design which could be installed lengthwise, as on the FN, or transversely, as on modern Hondas, Kawasakis, etc. The Binks reappeared a year later in an extremely neat London-built 'one-off' called the Evart-Hall, with fully enclosed chain drive and bucket seat, but regrettably this never went into production.

**(Below left): With three people to haul, this 1903 Humber with unusual Mills & Fullford double sidecars was hard-worked. (Below): Belgium's 4-cylinder shaft-drive FN brought new luxury standards to motorcycling in 1905. The example shown embodies a 2-speed gear in the final drive, introduced in 1910. 1 Pedal starting gear. 2 Carburettor. 3 Gear change lever. 4 Acetylene lamp. 5 Fork springs. 6 Fork links. 7 Magneto. 8 Overhead inlet & side exhaust valves. 9 Connecting rod & Piston. 10 Exhaust, silencer. 11 Crankshaft. 12 Flywheel & clutch. 13 Shaft drive. 14 2 speed gear. 15 Expanding brake.**

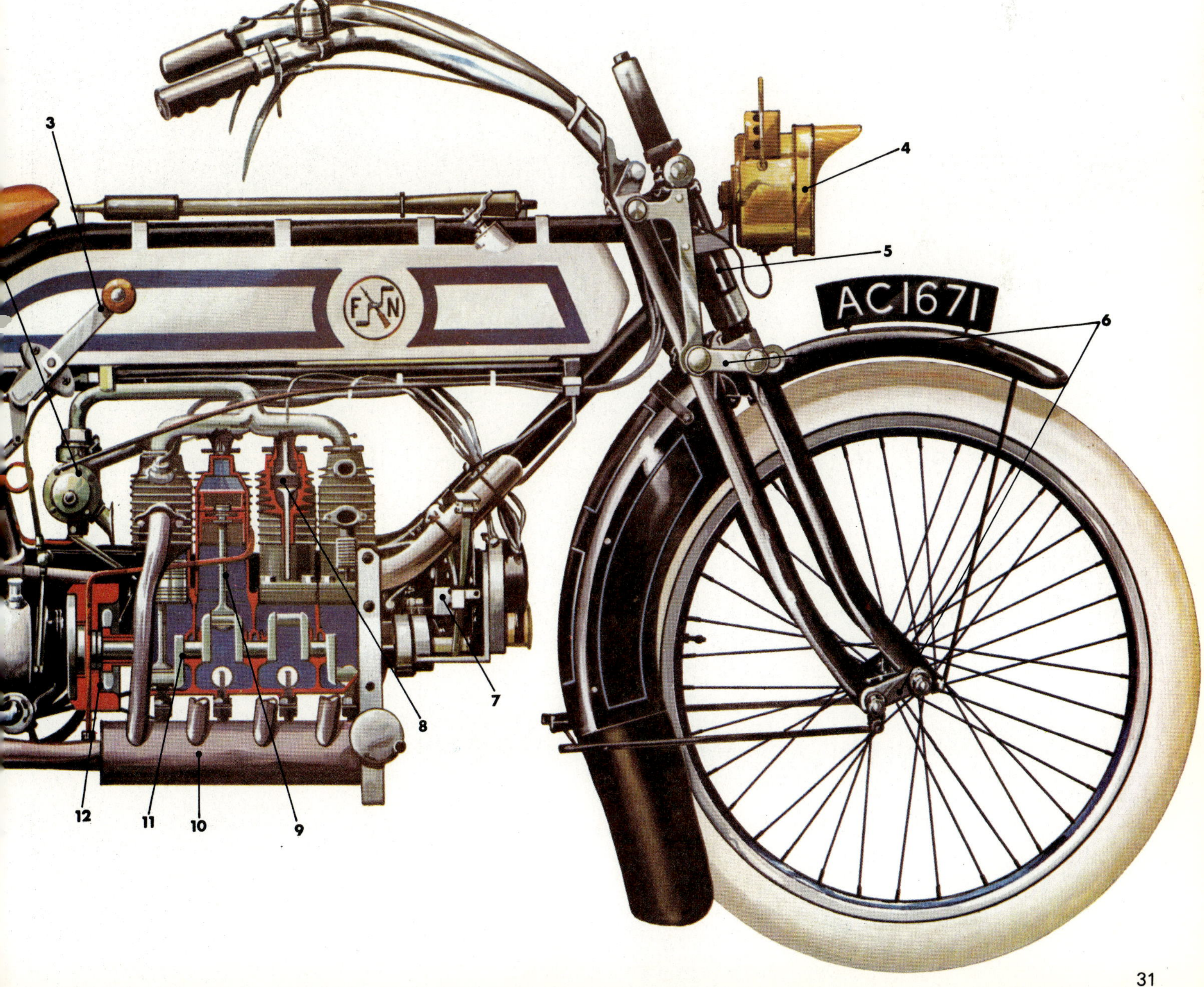

In Austria-Hungary (later Czechoslovakia) the go-ahead Laurin-Klement marque also built a 'four', a ponderous 5hp in-line design with clutch and chain drive, in 1905, while in Italy a future Fiat technical chief, Giulio Cappa, showed an ultramodern watercooled single with three-speed gearbox and shaft drive at the 1905 Turin *Salone*. In the United States, George Hendee took the obvious step of adding another cylinder to his rearward inclined single cylinder Indian, making a vee-twin and starting an irrevocable trend in American motorcycles.

In Bristol, in the south west of England, Joseph Barter of Light Motors Ltd exploited yet another layout employing twin horizontally opposed aircooled cylinders, which gave balanced firing periods and smooth torque, and occupied little height in the frame of the motorcycle.

Barter called his 1905 machine the *Fée*, then Anglicized it to the Fairy. It had a 200cc engine with automatic inlet valves, a friction clutch and belt drive, and engine parts were made for him by another Bristol firm, Douglas Brothers. When Barter ran out of money in 1907 he sold his flat twin to the Douglases. The design was further perfected and within a few years the Douglas motorcycle, with its characteristic flywheel, gentle 'phut-phut' exhaust note and blue and silver tank had become a familiar sight on British roads, having the virtues of flexibility, relative silence and reliability. The self-same engine layout is equally familiar today, installed transversely in the world famous German BMW.

Further evidence that there is little new under the sun came from France and Belgium, again in 1905, when the illustrious Werner brothers and the Brussels-built Bercley both introduced aircooled vertical twin engines. The Werner was made in $3\frac{1}{4}$ and 4hp sizes, while the 616cc Bercley, designed by Gustave Kindermann, had a three-bearing 'coincident' crankshaft with the pistons moving up and down together, as on the modern vertical twin. Neither of these antecedents lasted long, unfortunately; the Werner business faltered with the premature death of Michel in 1905 and finally closed down in 1908; while Bercley also had gone by 1909.

As with the automobile, so the early motorcycle benefitted vitally from the acid test of road racing. At first motorcycles ran as poor relations in the great town-to-town races, being largely overshadowed by their bigger, more glamorous four-wheeled brethren. Moreover, the so-called 'motorcycle' class did not differentiate between two- and three-wheelers, and many of the early 'motorcycle'

**Forerunner of the modern vertical twin, the 396cc two-cylinder Werner with overhead inlet valves, 1905. Pioneer of the horizontally-opposed 'flat-twin' engine, the first 340cc $2\frac{3}{4}$hp Douglas of 1907 was itself derived from Fée and Fairy designs. (Right): A later Douglas with countershaft gearbox and an early Scott twin 2-stroke feature in this intriguing glimpse of a motorcycle workshop.**

National Motor Museum

Motorcycle

National Motor Museum

victories fell to De Dion-Bouton and other tricycles powered by big 7 or 8hp engines.

As the three-wheeled anachronisms faded out in the first years of the new century, however, French two-wheelers such as Buchet, Clément and Werner came to the fore. Elie Buchet of Levallois was one of the first engineers to appreciate the value of high compression and ample valve area, and the Buchet racing motorcycle which succeeded his tricycles scored many successes up to 1902. The Clément, an offshoot of the car concern, took its share of spoils too, but the 'New Werner' with central engine location sensationally outshone them both, winning the two-wheel classes in the Paris-Bordeaux and Paris-Berlin races of 1901, the *Circuit du Nord* and Paris-Vienna in 1902, and the attenuated Paris-Madrid in 1903.

The latter was the event in which accidents were so numerous that the authorities terminated the race at Bordeaux. Racing on two, three or four wheels thereafter was confined to closed and policed circuits. The first 'classic' under these conditions, International Cup race, took place in 1904. As a kind of 'Gordon Bennett' or Grand Prix contest for all nations, it brought confrontation between the growing British motorcycle industry, the long-established French, and the Germans and Austrians. The seasoned Griffon machines from France placed first, third and fourth, with Austrian Laurin-Klements second and fifth, while the British entries, a Quadrant, a Lagonda and a JAP, were all knocked out by punctures from nails deliberately strewn on the course by saboteurs; the race was eventually declared null and void.

The event was held again in 1905, this time without outside interference, and an Austrian twin-cylinder Laurin-Klement won from a French Peugeot. British riders on Ariel, Matchless and JAP machines all retired, as did the Progress trio from Germany. If Britain still lacked the stamina to win, her industry was forging strongly ahead to future pre-eminence, whereas the German makers lacked the genius of their car compatriots. Austria won again in the third and last International Cup, this time with a pair of twin-cylinder Puch machines which took the first two places ahead of a British Matchless. The unsatisfactory nature of these three Continental races caused much discontent among the British, and precipitated the inauguration a year later of the now world-famous Isle of Man 'TT' (Tourist Trophy) series.

Radio Times Hulton

Brooklands track, designed by the same Colonel Holden who invented the four-cylinder motorcycle in 1897, had been opened in 1907, but was suitable for flat-out work only, whereas the Isle of Man offered roads, corners and hills in abundance, and proved an ideal 'forcing house' for design and development. The car TT race had been held there since 1905 and now, in 1907, came the first motorcycle TT, expressly for normal production machines. The long 37-mile Mountain course was deemed too hilly for 5hp gearless motorcycles, and the shorter 15.8-mile (25.4-km) St Johns circuit was therefore mapped out.

That first TT highlighted the shortcomings of belt drive, single speeds, inefficient engines, poor tires, and the futility of 'l.p.a.' on difficult sections. An ohv JAP-engined Matchless won the single-cylinder class at 38.2mph (61.5km/h), and a vee-twin Peugeot-engined Norton the multi-cylinder class at 36.22mph (58.3km/h). For the next year's race pedal gear was barred, and the first variable-geared motorcycles to compete, a pair of NSUs from Germany with epicyclic two-speed engine pulleys, ran without success. Two FN 'fours' with hand lever-operated clutches did better, one coming third in the multicylinder class, won by a 5hp vee-twin Dot. A side-valve Triumph was best single.

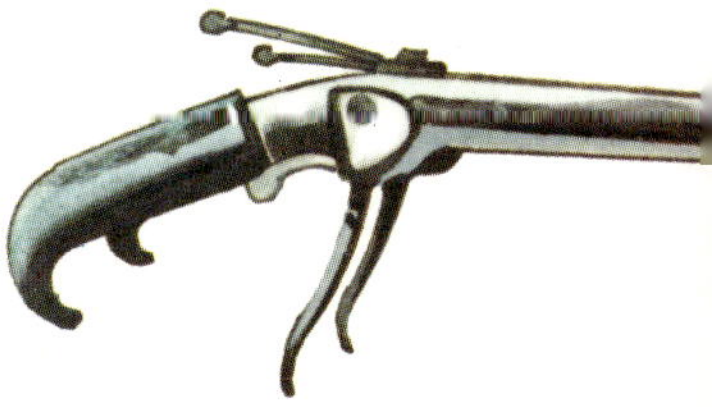

The 1909 and 1910 races saw disappointing progress in variable gear developments, but important advances elsewhere. Triumph of Coventry, by then very much the preeminent British marque, produced a 'free engine' device in 1909 comprising a hub-type clutch in the rear wheel. They also pioneered two-lever carburettor control by means of throttle and air levers on the handlebars, while in the same TT a significant new machine from Yorkshire made a literally quiet racing debut. This was the twin-cylinder two-stroke Scott, a motorcycle still revered today for its superb running, soft purr and flexibility.

Its designer was Alfred Scott of Bradford, who had experimented with twin-cylinder two-strokes since 1902, and by 1908 had attained the production point. His new motorcycle was a revelation in neatness and originality. Instead of the customary diamond or triangular frame and 'New Werner' engine position, Scott's parallel twin engine was inclined forward between a neat open duplex triangulated frame which strongly recalled the Hildebrand & Wolfmuller of 14 years earlier. The engine measured 58×63mm (333cc), had deflector-type pistons on 180° cranks, and watercooled cylinder heads, with the radiator above on the frame.

Drive to the rear wheel was via a P. & M.-style two-speed all-chain transmission, with rocking pedal foot gearchange. A cylindrical petrol tank was mounted on the saddle tube above the 'gears', and this radical design also had telescopic front forks working through guides, with a single central enclosed spring. In the fashion of the time, Alfred Scott's first road machine was fitted with aesthetically deplorable but physically comfortable 'sit up and beg' handlebars, but the 1909 TT Scott with racing bars looked lean, low and purposeful.

It embodied another 'first', a practical kickstarter formed from a crank which spun the engine through a length of chain. Its efficacy at the start brought the following comment in *Motor Cycling's* report of the race:

> "At the words 'Get Ready' Myers stamped on the starting pedal and the Scott fired at once; at the word 'Go' he was moving away in the saddle before the man starting with him had hardly begun to run. It served to show the public how a motorcycle should be started."

As so often happens with a new design, Scott's first TT effort ended in retirement, but eventually this brilliant and beautiful machine found reliability to match its pace and won the 500cc Senior TT twice in succession, in 1912 and 1913.

The fruitful year of 1908 brought other

**(Left): All sorts and sizes of motorcycle gathered in the yard of the Chequers Inn, Uxbridge, before one of the Auto Cycle Union's Quarterly reliability trials in 1910. (Below): One of the most brilliant British designs of all time was the twin-cylinder 2-stroke watercooled Scott, seen here in 1913 form. Designed by Alfred Scott of Bradford, Yorks., and introduced in late 1908, its specification included 2-speed gear with rocking pedal operating both gears and clutch, all-chain drive, kickstarter, telescopic front forks and open. duplex frame. (Below): An overhead view of the Scott, showing the control layout. 1 Windshield. 2 Magneto control. 3 Half-compression lever. 4 Foot brake. 5 Spring footboard. 6 Carrier. 7 Water tank. 8 Radiator. 9 Throttle. 10 Air control. 11 Petrol tank. 12 Oil filler. 13 Gear-change pedal. 14 Starter. 15 Tool box.**

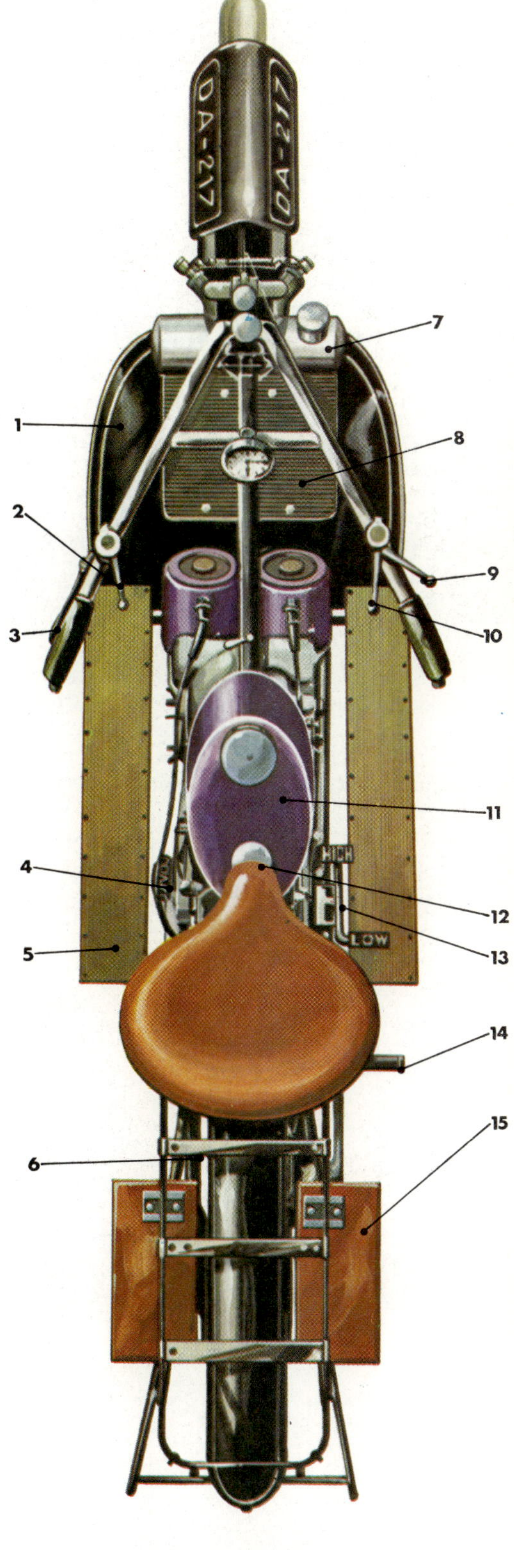

National Motor Museum

**(Left): America's first big 4-cylinder was the Pierce of 1909. This restored example has too modern a saddle but is otherwise basically authentic. (Below): The remarkable 4-cylinder Wilkinson-TMC, introduced in 1909 as a 'car on 2 wheels' by the famous English swordsmiths, with spring frame, shaft drive, two hub brakes and a bucket seat. (Right): The spectacular 2 litre V8-engined machine with which the American Glenn Curtiss attacked records in Florida. (Bottom right): The British-built Zenith Zenette, introduced in 1907, had a 500cc Fafnir side-valve engine, and was available early in 1908 with the famous Zenith 'Gradua' variable gear, an expanding engine pulley and sliding rear wheel spindle.**

innovations. There were several spring frames and forks, and an 'infinitely variable' belt drive called the Gradua, introduced on a motorcycle designed by F. W. Barnes and called the Zenette, which became the Zenith a year later. This drive was crude but remarkably effective, consisting simply of an expanding engine pulley and a movable rear wheel spindle, drawn forward or back in guides by hand winder gear on the tank, and providing infinite variation between about $3\frac{1}{2}$ and $7\frac{1}{2}$ to 1 ratios. So well did it work, in conjunction with a lusty twin-cylinder engine, that the Zenith proved unbeatable in hillclimb and sprint events, and was accordingly banned from 'single gear' classes by many major clubs. The makers exploited this to the full by adopting a 'barred' trade mark on their badge.

## Busy America

Across the Atlantic, rugged road conditions had seen the first motorcycles evolve into husky, powerful machines with twin-cylinder engines outnumbering the singles. Spectacular news filtered across of a fantastic multi-cylinder device on which Glenn Curtiss, later famous in connection with Curtiss aircraft, attacked the motorcycle speed record in 1907. His machine had a 2-litre V8 engine with air-cooled separate cylinders at 90°, giving 40bhp which was transmitted by shaft to the rear wheel. This unit was intended for an experimental flying machine but Curtiss installed it in a long, trussed Marvel motorcycle frame for testing. At Daytona Beach, Florida, he unleashed it along a four-mile stretch of sand and passed through a measured flying mile in a claimed 26.4 seconds. This gave an astonishing 137mph (220km/h) which was frankly disbelieved by many and was never officially recognized.

More practical was America's first 'four', introduced in 1909 by the makers of the top-quality Pierce-Arrow car. Called simply the Pierce, it followed FN practice with four separate in-line aircooled cylinders, and shaft final drive, but the engine was a T-head with inlet valves on one side and exhaust on the other, with two separate camshafts. The frame top member and fore and aft down-tubes were formed in broad $3\frac{1}{2}$in-diameter steel tubing, which also served as fuel and oil tanks, and in 1910 two-speed transmission with a multiple disc clutch was added, making the Pierce superbly tractable. Unfortunately it was consistently produced at a loss, although the $400 price would almost buy a Model T Ford car, and production ceased in 1913.

## 'Dream machine'

A similar fate attended another four-cylinder 'dream machine', built in Britain by Wilkinson-TMC of Acton, London, an off-shoot of the famous Wilkinson Sword Company. In 1909 they had built a prototype 'car on two wheels' with transverse-mounted twin-cylinder engine, underslung worm shaft drive, cantilever leaf-sprung frame, hub brakes front and rear, a steering wheel, bucket seat and generous enclosure. An improved version with 678cc in-line four-cylinder engine followed, and during subsequent development it acquired an 848cc watercooled engine with mechanically operated valves, emerging as an extremely comfortable and luxurious machine. Too long, too heavy, too complicated and too expensive was, however, the harsh verdict, and one more 'ideal' had gone by 1913.

National Motor Museum

World's Record – Ormond Beach, Fla.
1 Mile – 26 2/5 Seconds.
8 Cylinder, 40 H. P. Motor Cycle
Built by The Curtiss Manufacturing Company, Hammondsport, N. Y.

National Motor Museum

National Motor Museum

Radio Times Hulton

Six up, and all's well (left): A Premier sidecar outfit which climbed River Hill, Sevenoaks, in 1913 with six passengers aboard.
(Below): Brutal transition for men, women, motors and motorcycles came with the Great War in 1914; this 1918 scene depicts the unbelievable changes wrought in four years, with a woman dispatch rider on her RAF P & M 'sloper' combination passing a staff car with woman chauffeur.
(Top right): A popular British all-rounder in pre-Great War years was the rugged, reliable belt-drive 3½hp, 500cc side-valve Triumph with 'free engine' clutch drive.

In 1910 the 'free engine' or clutched drive, became all the rage. Many and varied were the devices, some with the clutch in the rear hub, others on the belt pulley or the engine shaft. With a single speed having a 'compromise' ratio of, say, 4½ to 1, however, getaway was hard on belt-fasteners, which all too easily pulled out. Obviously the separate gearbox with two or even three speeds just had to come soon, followed ultimately by chain drive, but meantime the 'free engine' was sufficient novelty for conservative manufacturers and motorcyclists.

It may amaze today's 'bikers' with their sweet clutches and five or six speeds, but in 1910 even an advanced make like Indian in the United States proudly advertised: "Our free engine clutch is a revelation in motorcycle construction—you can start anywhere and run at any speed. You can stop anywhere without stopping the engine." BSA, an important British newcomer that year, charged £6 10s extra for their 'free engine', while Matchless advertised an 'extra', their adjustable engine pulley—"a practical substitute for a two-speed gear at one-tenth the cost . . . gear changed in 20 seconds including adjusting length of belt without use of spanners or tools."

The pros and cons of variable gears dominated the first Olympia Show in London exclusive to motorcycles, held late in 1910 attended by 80 000 visitors. A total of 390 models were gathered there, among them a new lightweight Royal Enfield twin with Motosacoche vee-engine distinguished by its horizontal cooling fins, and P. & M.-type two-speed gear. Nortons showed their 633cc 'Big Four' single with a Norton-made Roc two-speed rear hub gear; the two-speed Scott was there, also an advanced Lea-Francis with two-speed gearbox and fully enclosed chain drive, while Sidney Horstman from Bath, later a car manufacturer, featured a neat two-speed conversion for the four-cylinder FN.

Important high quality newcomers from the cycle trade included Rudge-Whitworth with a 3½hp, 499cc model having pushrod-operated inlet valve over the exhaust (i.o.e.), and the Stevens-engined two-speed Clyno. Variation on the motorized bicycle theme came in the 118cc Wall 'Autowheel', an outboard unit clipped to one side of the rear wheel. There were several new sprung front forks, and an outbreak of abortive rotary valve designs as a change from the time-proven poppet type.

While Britain's motorcycle industry waxed strongly, morale on the European Continent had waned. France, once the leader, showed a preference for small cars and cycle-cars, their two-wheelers advancing little. Peugeot and Magnat-Debon changed over from automatic to mechanical inlet valves, and there

# BUSY DECADE

"The motor-bicycle is now a vehicle suited for old and young, strong and weak . . ."
*Motor Cycling,* 1912

National Motor Museum

Imperial War Museum

were some clever frame-springing devices, but belt drive and clutchless single-speeds remained the norm.

Germany, too, seemed much absorbed with the motor car, although NSU Wanderer, Allright and Brennabor catered for both two and four wheels, and the weird engine-over-front wheel Phanomen for three as well. 'Germania' machines from Dresden were Austrian Laurin-Klements built under licence, but among sound domestic products were the Hercules and Victoria, both built in Nuremberg, while the versatile Hans Grade, pioneer pilot, race driver and designer, dabbled with variable gears on his well-made motorcycles.

In Italy the Frera, Della Ferrera and Fongri were substantial but conventional 500s reared for rugged local conditions, while interesting rivals included the Moto-Borgo, built by two Turin brothers later famous for their light alloy pistons, and the Siamt, an advanced vee-twin with pushrod ohv and sporting performance. Holland contributed a machine called the Vulkaan with Swiss-made Zedel engine, and the Swedish Rex used a Motosacoche unit. A certain irony attaches to the appearance in 1910 on the Japanese market of a new domestic model called the Miyapet. The makers, from Otaku, Tokyo, reported a first year's output of 16 motorcycles—a modest harbinger of stupendous things to come 60 years later!

If 1910 was the year of the 'free engine', 1911 was the year of variable gears—and curiously it was road racing that forced the issue and compelled the industry to take action. In four short years the Isle of Man TT had become the world's most important motorcycle race, and when the organizers, the Auto-Cycle Union, decided to stiffen conditions in 1911 they did it by changing from the old 16-mile St Johns course to the full $37\frac{3}{4}$-mile 'Mountain' circuit used by the cars.

This caused a tremendous flutter among prospective entrants, for the long course included many tight corners, hilly sections, and a long, rough 6-mile uphill grind from Ramsey to the side of Snaefell mountain (2034 ft), all of which made variable gears imperative.

National Motor Museum

National Motor Museum

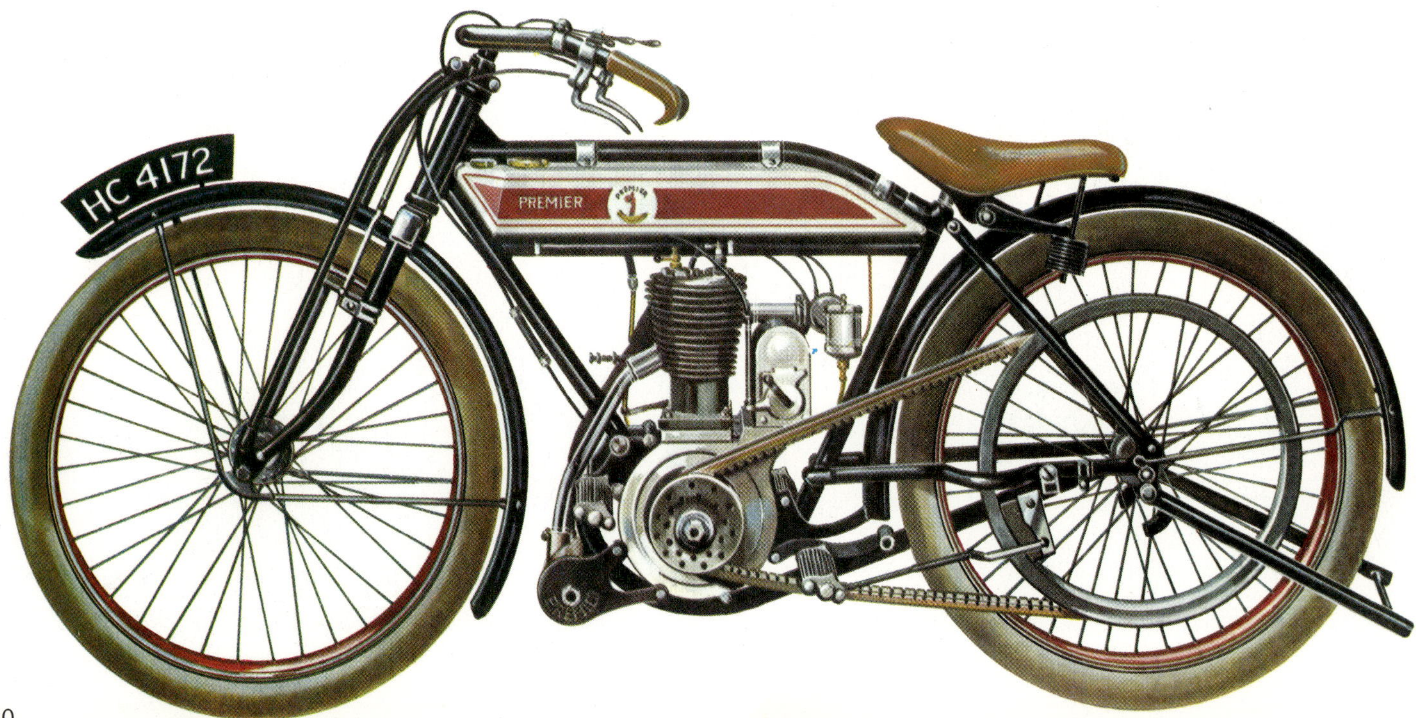

Rear hub epicyclic two or three speeds of beefed-up cycle type with belt drive were used by most runners, one exception being the Zenith Gradua. Another was a new and speedily devised variation on the same system evolved by Rudge, in which both front and rear pulleys expanded or contracted in sympathy with each other, obviating the sliding rear wheel spindle.

But the British had the shock of their lives when three 585cc vee-twin Indian machines from America absolutely hogged the Senior TT, taking the first three places! These foreign usurpers had two-speed countershaft gearboxes and all-chain drive, giving double emphasis that it was high time motorcycle transmissions in Europe were modernized. From then on the single-speeder was doomed, save only in the small economy lightweight class, and at the 1911 Olympia Show, 83 per cent of the 275 different motorcycles exhibited offered variable gears of some kind.

Armstrong, Millennium and Sturmey-Archer hub gears were popular for their easy adaption to the old-type single-speeders, but bottom bracket gears were also in demand, while Rudge had a production version of their TT expanding pulley gear, calling it the Multi. It remained clear, however, that makers would have to go the whole hog and fit countershaft gearboxes behind the engine, and Douglas, for one, gave their popular flat-twins more than a facelift, fitting a countershaft two-speed gearbox following lathe backgear 'tumbler' principles; a clutch and kick starter were optional extras, clutchless starts being effected in time-honoured manner with the exhaust valve lifter.

### The Sunbeam tradition

The thriving new AJS concern marketed a big twin with three-speed and kick-starter, but probably the most important exhibit of all was the first motorcycle to bear the august name of Sunbeam. Marketed by the John Marston Company, the new Sunbeam epitomized all that the phrase 'Made in England' meant in those far off days when British workmanship and finish were unmatched anywhere in the world. Established Sunbeam products such as their bicycles and cars had very fine reputations and the motorcycle carried on this 'nothing but the best' tradition.

**(Top left): The Rudge Multi transmission, introduced in 1911, employed two expanding belt pulleys. This is a 1920 model. (Below left): The Wall 'Autowheel', a tiny engine/wheel unit clamped to the side of an ordinary pedal cycle, about to undergo a gruelling test. (Bottom left): Typifying the belt drive, single-speed machine of pre-Great War days—the 1912 499cc side valve Premier, with special auxiliary exhaust valve to improve engine scavenging, necessitating a second exhaust pipe. (Below right): The Douglas 2-speed transmission introduced in 1910. (Below): The rugged 1914 AJS big twin with sidecar provided excellent family transport.**

*National Motor Museum*

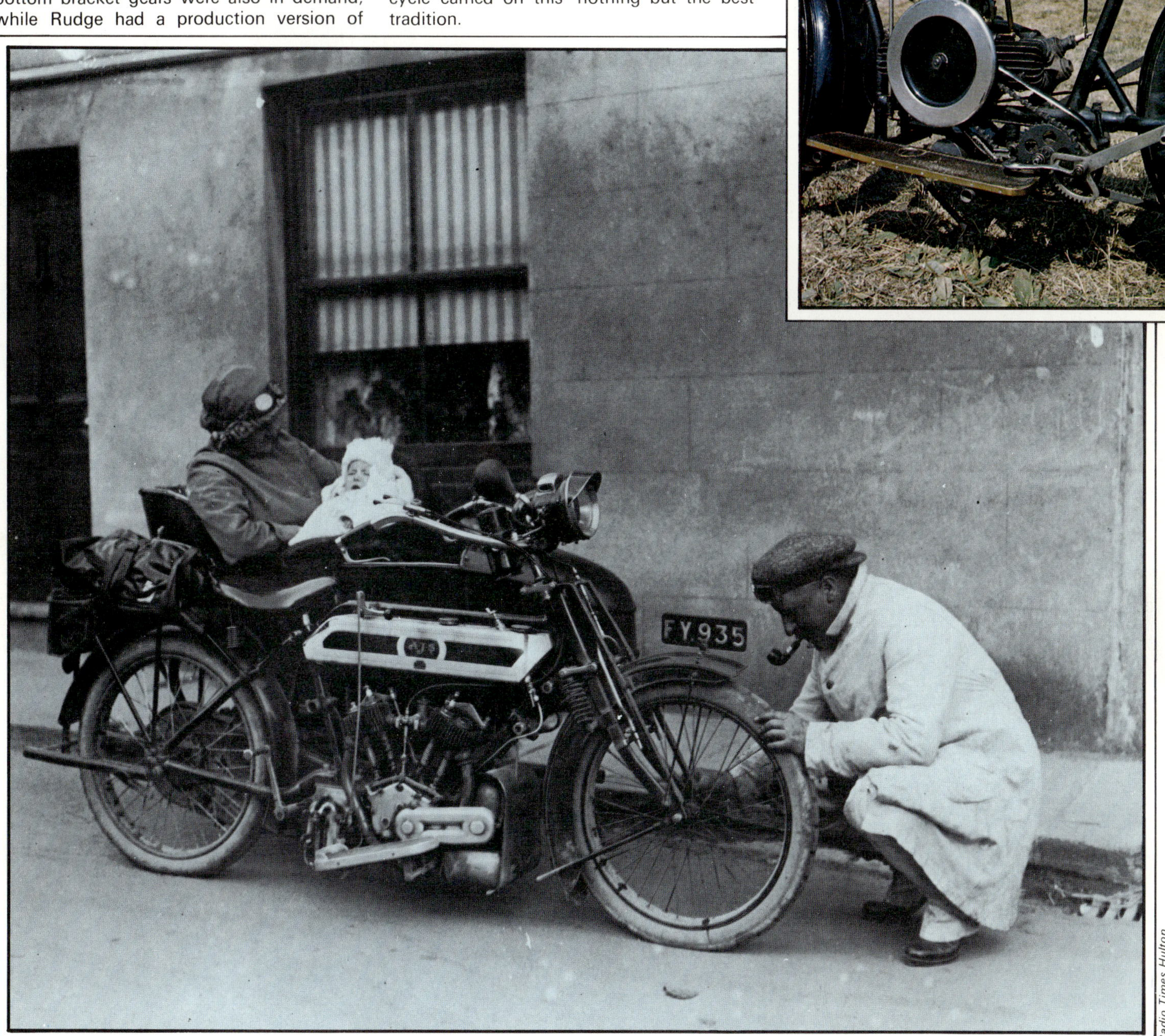


*Radio Times Hulton*

Design-wise it was up-to-the-minute in 1912 in having two-speed countershaft gearbox with kick-start and all-chain drive, with both primary and final chains enclosed in an oil bath bearing the brand name 'The Little Oil Bath', already famous on Sunbeam cycles. The engine was a 75×79mm, 349cc $2\frac{3}{4}$hp side-valve, and the clutch was cable and lever controlled from the handlebar. Built to such 'Rolls-Royce' standards, it seemed surprising for the Sunbeam to be raced, yet it was, and highly successfully. The larger 499cc $3\frac{1}{2}$hp model produced in 1913 showed its mettle in the 1914 Senior TT by deadheating for second place with an Indian twin, and basically the same side-valve design won many classic road races just after the First World War.

Yet not even the advanced new Sunbeam, nor America's overwhelming 1911 TT twin, nor a soaking wet 1912 TT which highlighted the grave disadvantage of slipping belts, were sufficient to precipitate a rush to all-chain drive. Most manufacturers cautiously compromised with chain-cum-belt, i.e. chain primary drive and a gearbox with a pulley for the belt rear drive. Nonetheless emancipation from the 'push and hop on' start had come about at last, and riders of motorcycles with a clutch and two gears in the last halcyon days before the First World War wondered how they had survived without these adjuncts.

Meanwhile in the United States, which had helped cause this design upheaval, the motorcycle industry was also enjoying a boom. From their curious rear-inclined singles produced early in the century, by 1912 the United States had become the land of the big twin. Vast land tracts and surprisingly primitive and undeveloped roads had bred powerful, sturdy machines with Indian and Harley-Davidson to the forefront. As in Europe, proprietary engines, clutches and other parts encouraged new makes; prominent engine builders were Thor of Illinois, F. W. Spacke of Indiana, and Joerns-Thiem of Minnesota, who also made two-speed hubs.

### Vee-twins

Until 1914 American single-cylinder models with belt drive were still marketed, although by that time vee-twins preponderated, with makes such as Jefferson, Michaelson, De Luxe, AMC, Dayton, Monarch, Pope, Pirate, Reading-Standard, Yale and Excelsior all prominent. Belts could not withstand the power from husky engines of between 750 and over 1000cc, and chain drive soon became the rule, apart from Peerless of Boston and Feilbach of Milwaukee, who both followed Pierce's earlier example and offered shaft drive.

Other mechanical novelties abounded. The Militaire was a curious device with underslung tubular chassis, low-pivot steering, artillery wheels, shaft drive, three-speed gearbox, a spring frame with side support wheels like Daimler's original motorcycle of 1885, and a choice of single or four-cylinder engines! Another odd 'four' was the first Henderson of 1911, which had a curved cradle giving needlessly long wheelbase and an empty space, occupied by full-width footboards, ahead of the 1068cc ohiv engine. The creator, expatriate Scotsman William Henderson, had second thoughts and later Henderson 'fours' had side valves in a normal length frame, and were built throughout the 1920s. No US two-wheeler of pre-1914 was more fantastic, however, than the Biautogo of 1913, built by James Scripps-Booth of Detroit. It was a gargantuan attempt at a two-wheeled car, with a wheelbase of 11ft 8in—longer than the contemporary Cadillac car!—and a specially constructed $5\frac{1}{2}$ litre 90° V8 watercooled engine and four-speed gearbox. There was an underslung car-type chassis of pressed steel, wheel steering, and an open tourer body seating the driver centrally, with room for two passengers behind him, side by

side on a bench seat. Twin pairs of small retractable side support wheels were fitted, and the total weight without occupants was 3150lb! Workmanship was impressive, but not surprisingly only the very expensive prototype was built.

More practical and no less exciting was the bright yellow-painted Cyclone 1000cc twin, which in 1913 had bevel-driven overhead camshaft (ohc) heads with inclined valves, domed pistons and roller-cum-ball big end bearings—and a reputation for over 100-mph (160-km) performance, borne out in several 1914 races. Another famous 'wearer of the yellow' was the Flying Merkel, typifying the lusty US big twin, but with a neatly sprung frame incorporating a central enclosed coil spring under the saddle, telescopic front forks and an oil reservoir formed from part of the frame.

**(Left): Yankee stalwart—the indefatigable Harley-Davidson vee-twin in 1915 form with sidecar. (Top right): 100mph was claimed in 1913 for the exciting 1000cc big twin Cyclone with overhead camshaft engine. (Below right): The 2-wheeled car theme was taken to the extremes of using a steering wheel and artillery wheels on the first single-cylinder American Militaire of 1910. They soon reverted to handle-bars, and fitted a 4-cylinder engine and shaft drive, but heavy cost killed the venture.**

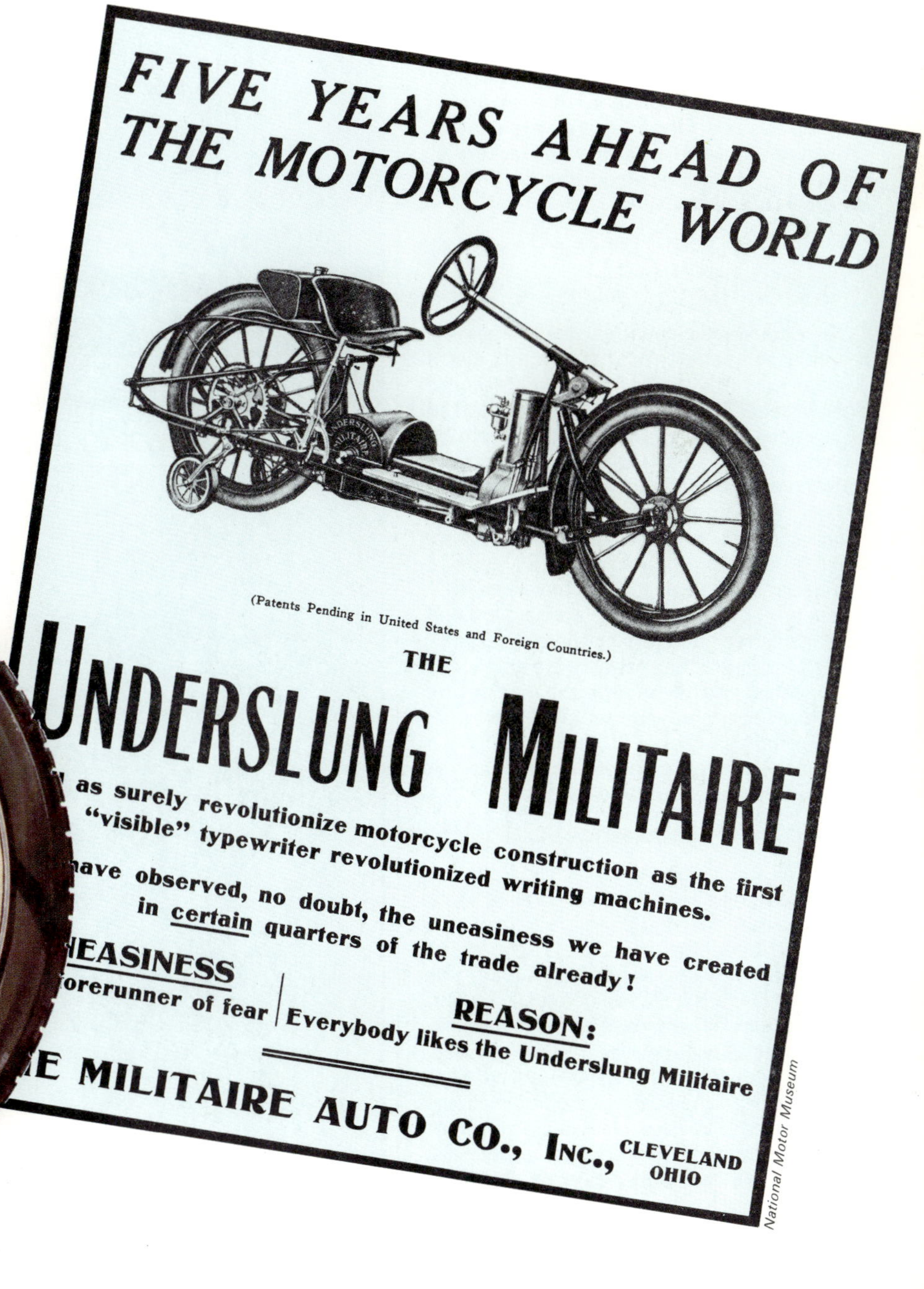

FIVE YEARS AHEAD OF THE MOTORCYCLE WORLD

(Patents Pending in United States and Foreign Countries.)

THE

UNDERSLUNG MILITAIRE

l as surely revolutionize motorcycle construction as the first "visible" typewriter revolutionized writing machines.

ave observed, no doubt, the uneasiness we have created in certain quarters of the trade already!

IEASINESS

orerunner of fear

REASON:

Everybody likes the Underslung Militaire

E MILITAIRE AUTO CO., INC., CLEVELAND OHIO

National Motor Museum

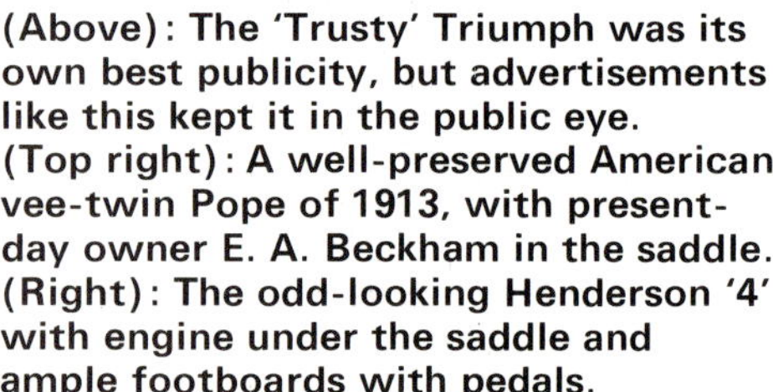

**(Above): The 'Trusty' Triumph was its own best publicity, but advertisements like this kept it in the public eye. (Top right): A well-preserved American vee-twin Pope of 1913, with present-day owner E. A. Beckham in the saddle. (Right): The odd-looking Henderson '4' with engine under the saddle and ample footboards with pedals.**

National Motor Museum

Radio Times Hulton

National Motor Museum

An extra sophistication on the Merkel was a spring self-starter. Twelve months later it was capped by Indian with their Hendee Special superbike with electric starter, worked by a chain-driven motor-generator and two six-volt batteries. The idea was dropped in 1915 as being too far ahead of its time. . . .

The Wisconsin-built Jefferson was a pushrod ohv twin which did well in racing, while a rival, the Pope, had an early form of plunger rear springing, differing from later practice in pulling the coil springs through links instead of compressing them. Aesthetically, all these fine Americans were spoiled by the then fashionable but unsightly 'sit up and beg' handlebars, which sprouted back from the steering head about 2ft, giving the rider a comfortable if breezy upright position at cost of considerable extra frontal area.

### Pedal change

Several side-valve big twins also appeared in Europe at that time, the sidecar being much in vogue but demanding more power and flexibility than the average single could reasonably provide. Not every single was 'average', of course, Excelsior actually making one of 800cc! There were some interesting lightweight developments; a new make, Levis, introduced a 211cc two-speed two-stroke model, while 292cc proprietary four-strokes were marketed by Veloce, the fore-runners of the famous Velocette, and Villiers, an offshoot of the John Marston Company which owned Sunbeam. Both engines had two-speed unit construction gearboxes, while the Veloce also had a pedal change—harbinger of a future 'must'.

The stimulating 1910–14 period, so rich in technical developments, was arrested with startling suddenness when Germany marched into Belgium and the First World War engulfed Western civilization. The motorcycle followed man into uniform and proved its value and versatility to the world. In the First World War there was no telephone network for communication in the battle areas, and countless vital messages had to be rushed by dispatch riders. In earlier wars their mount had been the horse; in 1914–18 it became the motorcycle.

## Commandeered

At first civilian machines were commandeered, most of them perishing in the appalling conditions in the battle areas, where roads and tracks were destroyed. Soon several famous makers had switched their production entirely to dispatch rider (DR) motorcycles. For messenger work the British army chose 350cc flat-twin Douglases and 500cc Triumph singles, the latter with a new Sturmey-Archer countershaft three-speed gearbox, while for machine gun mounts bigger two-cylinder Royal Enfields, Clynos, Scotts, etc were employed. Other makers which served 'under the colours' included BSA, New Imperial, AJS, Sunbeam and James.

The Royal Flying Corps, later the Royal Air Force, selected the 500cc 'sloper' P. & M., the Belgians favoured FNs and Douglases, the French army used Peugeot, Terrot and Réné-Gillet, the Italians had Bianchis, Freras, Garellis, etc, the Americans brought over Harley-Davidson, Excelsior and Indian sidecar outfits and also Henderson 4s, the Germans used NSU, Wanderer, Victoria and other makes, while the Austrians had the Laurin-Klement and a mixture of 'conscripted' civilian models.

**(Bottom left): Ancestor of a famous line of British motorcycles, the 1913, $2\frac{1}{4}$hp Velocette with 206cc 2-stroke engine and two speeds. (Below): The motorcycle goes to war: A training scene during the Great War, with a 'Trusty' Triumph Model H solo in the foreground, and two columns of mobile gunners on Clyno sidecar outfits passing.**

Camera Press/Imperial War Museum

The major factories being fully occupied, several obscure British makes enjoyed a brief, unexpected prosperity in meeting civilian demand for motorcycles before manufacture was finally stopped by the authorities in 1916. Most of them took the easy road and fitted proprietary engines such as Villiers, Peco, Dalm or Metro two-strokes, or JAP, Precision or Blackburne four-strokes. Some very unfamiliar names came forward, such as Aeolus, Gaby, Raynal, Hockley and Elmdon from Birmingham, the London-built Juno and Burford, and the deplorably named Kumfurt, which came from Bedfordshire. Even the island of Guernsey contributed one, the light-weight open-framed JES-engined Ladies-Pacer, while a modest 210cc two-stroke from a Birmingham backstreet carried the portentious name Dispatch Rider, its inspiring tank transfer depicting a front-line DR storming through shot and shell!

Mary Evans

L. Shelley

Recalling Michaux-Perreaux days, a steam motorcycle, the Pearson & Cox, was revived in an effort to circumvent petrol restrictions, while some combinations towed trailers bearing huge gasbags to run on coal-gas. In those grim days many a nimble mechanical mind must have dwelt on the 'ideal' motorcycle during quiet moments; the basic elements of several were, indeed, laid down during the war. When at last the fighting was over and the Armistice signed, the eager dreamers set out to scrape up some cash to add to their service gratuities and turn their dreams into metal. And other eager thousands, now with firsthand knowledge of the value and pleasure of motorcycling, had *their* gratuities ready also, to buy a machine as soon as one became available.

**Service machines: (Far left): A British sidecar-mounted Maxim gun, depicted on a cigarette card. (Top left): An RFC P & M 'sloper' in India. (Bottom left): A famous Army 'workhorse', the $2\frac{3}{4}$hp 349cc flat-twin Douglas with 2-speeds and belt final drive. (Top right): A German DR machine, the twin-cylinder Wanderer, as restored in Italy. (Bottom right): A German dispatch rider with his machine in Düsseldorf.**

L. Shelley

Camera Press

Change of use for a sidecar outfit in 1919 was to a taxi—the machine is a 500cc 'big single' 2-stroke Dunelt. (Right): Back to peace—hill-hunting with a Triumph combination. (Far right): Demonstrating the 175lb overall weight of the ingenious 1919 flat-twin 398cc ABC.

Motor Cycle

With hundreds of factories and employees switching over from armaments to peaceful products, 1919 was chaotic. Coal, iron and steel were in short supply, and firms anxious to resume motorcycle manufacture had to wait patiently for supplies of iron and aluminium castings, machined parts, pressings, tubing, steel strip, electrical parts and many other commodities. But advertisements lured with proclamations such as 'Not long now to wait for your new X . . . . . .', and 'Order your new Y . . . . . now', while secondhand dealers and auctioneers did a roaring trade with prewar models. Machines costing £40 new in 1914 would cost £140 well used five years later, while petrol, oil and tire prices rose alarmingly. Nobody grumbled much at first; the guns were silenced and it was peace.

There was a great mushrooming of new motorcycle enterprises, with over 50 new British makes alone in 1919, over 40 more in 1920, and many others in other countries. Some were launched by aircraft, engineering or armaments firms seeking new outlets for their factories; the Beardmore-Precision backed by the big British ship, locomotive and aircraft builders, for example, the French Gnome-Rhône by the famous rotary aero-engine makers, the revived ABC by Sopwith Aviation, the Martinsyde and the Blériot by English and French plane makers respectively.

Others were new ventures, like the Hawker by a famous flier and later aircraft manufacturer; some bore names eloquent of the spirit of the times—the Bulldog and the Defy-all, the Pax and the New Era. There was the Spartan and the De Luxe, the Wizard, the Viper, Whippet and Badger, and many, many more. Some were well capitalized, others represented one man's gratuity and savings invested in a backyard workshop. A few survived the next few stormy years, but many more went under.

The Dunelt was made by a steel firm still thriving in Sheffield today, Dunfold & Elliott Ltd. It had an unusual but effective 499cc two-stroke single-cylinder engine with light alloy head and a 'stepped' light alloy piston which gave a supercharging effect and contributed to a 'sloggability' ideal for sidecar work. Francis-Barnett, formed by the sons of the founders of Lea-Francis and the old Singer motorcycle firm, became famous for their two-stroke lightweights, while the Raleigh, product of the famous cycle makers, had a vigorous decade ahead of it.

### New Continentals

In France the Monet-Goyon, a kind of 'Renault' of two-wheelers, was founded around British Villiers engines and other parts. In Belgium the sturdy Gillet was born. In Italy the prewar Bianchi and Gilera marques were joined by the tough Benelli and the clever little 349cc Garelli two-stroke, with double pistons and single combustion chamber. This quickly rose to racing preeminence over the '350' four-strokes in the early 1920s, giving shocks all round with its speed. Even in Germany, defeated and impoverished as she was, the now world-famous DKW began life in Saxony as a bicycle with its tiny two-stroke power unit over the back wheel.

An Olympia Show was just squeezed into 1919, when it became apparent that the hub and engine shaft variable gears had really had their day, and the 'standard' new transmission comprised a primary chain to a countershaft two or three speed gearbox with clutch and kick starter, and belt or chain final drive, the latter gradually overtaking the former in popularity. Clyno announced a fine new 8hp big twin 'Peace' model with spring frame and enclosed chain drive, while Matchless produced their famous Model H 'Victory' big twin. Examples of this seemingly indestructible machine, designed for army war service, could still be seen around in the 1930s, being memorable if not 'distinguished' for their dismal khaki finish reminiscent of the war everyone wanted to forget.

Villiers did tremendous business supplying two-stroke engines to small assembly firms, electric lighting took a step forward when Lucas introduced their 'Magdyno' combined magneto and dynamo, and there were several new spring frames on luxury models. Things, indeed, seemed back to normal when, standing out from the welter of sound, almost dull orthodoxy, there came the inevitable nonconformist designs that always enlivened the Olympia Shows. One such in 1919 was the Redrup Radial, product of an ex-aircraft designer from Cardiff. Forgetful of the Millet and the Rivierre of decades earlier, its three-cylinder fan-cooled radial engine of 309cc was acclaimed as revolutionary. It had a three-speed gearbox and a dated and out-of-context belt drive; its career was brief.

A true 'dream bike' was the Superb Four, built in 1920 at Anerley in southeast London. This had an up-to-the-minute in-line four-cylinder engine in light alloy with single overhead camshaft, three speeds and chain drive, but its daring specification and price doomed it on a tough market where buyers would not risk their hard-won cash on something experimental or unknown. Also fated for a short life was the Doncaster-built Danum 'All Weather', an ultra-modern looking vehicle with full enclosure, disc wheels, a

Motor Cycle

Motor Cycle

Epitomizing the big post-War vee-twin, the London-built 995cc Matchless combination gained a great reputation for dependability in the '20s.

Motor Cycle

pressed steel frame, rear springing and shaft drive. The Pullin-Groom designed by Cyril Pullin lasted a bit longer; it too had full enclosure and pressed steel frame, and was powered by a horizontal single-cylinder engine.

### Ingenuity unavailing

But the most tragic demise of all was that of the ABC, a highly sophisticated design which drew big crowds at Olympia in 1919. A product of the All British Engine Company, born in 1913 but refloated with Sopwith capital after the war, it had a 68.6×54mm 398cc flat-twin inclined ohv engine, installed transversely in the frame (like the modern BMW) and in unit with a four-speed gearbox. Final drive was by chain, the clutch was twist-grip controlled, and the basic design was completed, it is said, in 11 days by Granville Bradshaw. Add $\frac{1}{4}$-elliptic leaf springing, internal expanding hub brakes front and rear, an overall weight of only 175lb, a smooth, silent and brisk performance, and there were all the makings of a working 'ideal'.

Alas, like so many dream designs before and since, the ABC failed. Forced by bulging order books and clamouring dealers into premature production before its design was properly developed and tested, many teething troubles were encountered. The pushrods and rocker gear were too frail, there were lubrication defects and the kickstart gave trouble. Granville Bradshaw slaved to remedy them, but meanwhile the chaotic supply of materials in 1919–20 added serious problems and costs spiralled until the market price stood at a daunting £160. Despite some striking race and record successes, including a French Grand Prix victory for the French 500cc edition built under licence by Gnome-et-Rhône, and a new hour class record at Brooklands, the Sopwith Company decided to cut their losses, and a potentially brilliant British design abruptly disappeared.

### 'The flying banana'

Doubtless inspired by the successful Douglas, there was a spate of other flat-twins besides the ill-fated ABC. Coventry Victor built a 688cc 'over the counter' unit which several makers used; Zenith made a '350' with their famous Gradua gear, Humber and Raleigh marketed luxury three-speed all-chain models, and Wooler of Alperton built a lively 350cc flat-twin distinguished by plunger springing on the fork extremities at front and

(Left): Danish police on a new domestic motorcycle, the remarkable 750cc 4-cylinder Nimbus built in Copenhagen from 1920 to 1957. (Right): Indestructible: This 1920 Indian 'Powerplus' 7/9hp side-valve vee-twin typifies the massive 'super-comfort' American motorcycle of the 1920s. (Below): Knees up for the rider, as a twin-cylinder Clyno combination ambles easily through a rural watersplash near Edgware, North London; today a busy arterial road crosses the site.

National Motor Museum

National Motor Museum

National Motor Museum

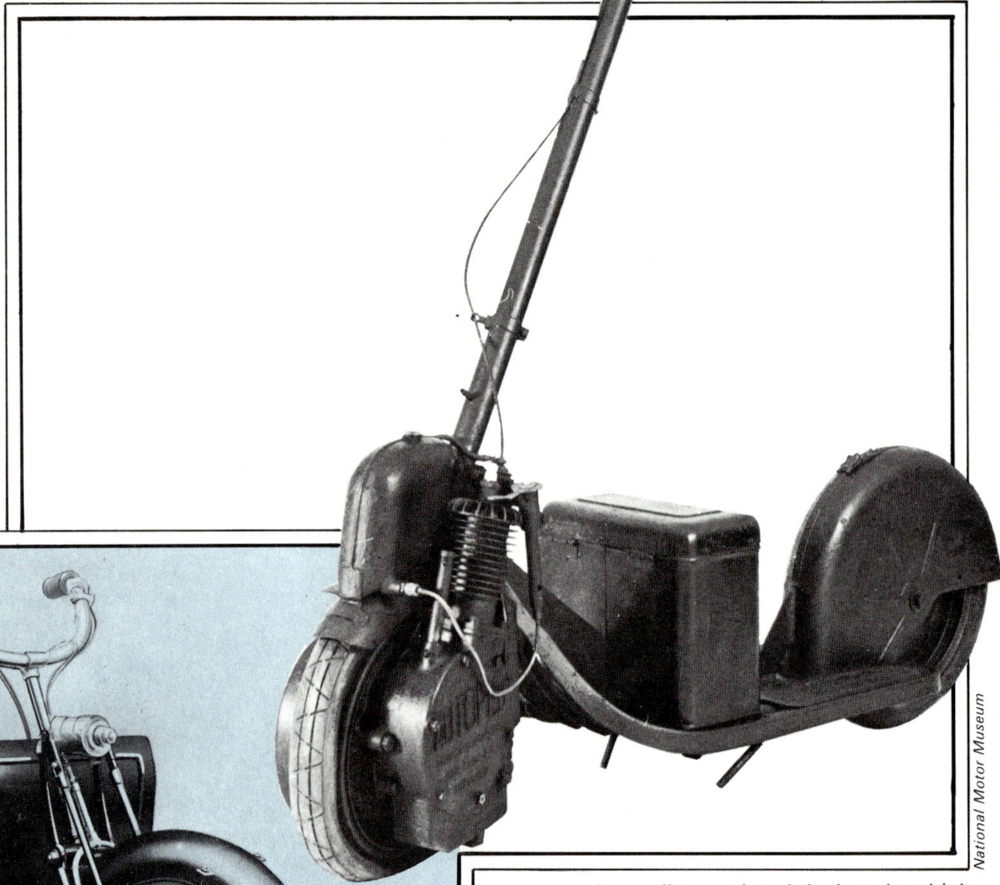
National Motor Museum

National Motor Museum

National Motor Museum

rear, and a yellow-painted fuel tank which projected forward around the steering head, earning it the nickname 'the flying banana'. Even Harley-Davidson of the United States, land of the big vee-twin, produced a 584cc horizontally-opposed model intended for solo work, marred as ever by the American insistence on 'sit up and beg' handlebars.

## The scooter bubble

Trying to keep their factory employed until transverse flat-twin production got under way, ABCs also involved themselves in that early postwar phenomenon, the scooter craze. Precipitated by an American wartime austerity device with small wheels and no saddle called the Autoped, the scooter was seized upon avidly as a cheaper form of mobility than even the lightweight motorcycle. Its role was that of a handy 'runabout' for local travel rather than long-distance work, with the most basic mechanicals and controls, and sufficient protection to be ridden in a lounge suit or the long skirt of the time.

Several scooters had no gears or seat, some were two-strokes, others had bijou four-stroke sv or ohv units, one was electric-powered, and most had small pressed wheels. Even DKW and Krupp of Germany built them. They were cheap but in too many cases regrettably nasty; exceptions included the Stafford built by the Alvis car concern, the 180cc ohv alloy-engined Whippet, ABC's 125cc ohv 'Skootamota', a luxury two-seater called the Reynolds Runabout, and Gloster Aircraft's Unibus, which had full enclosure, all round springing and worm drive. Good, bad or indifferent, the breed soon foundered on its own limitations, but reappeared over a quarter-century later in more efficient form.

However sensible it might be, austerity had small chance in the fervour of postwar revival,

(Top left and right): Precipitating the scooter craze of the early '20s, the deceptively neat and simple American Autoped first appeared in 1915 with 155cc 4-stroke engine. (Below left): Far more luxurious was the 1922 Reynolds Runabout with twin bucket seats, open frame and enclosed Liberty 2-stroke engine. (Bottom left): The ABC-built Skootamota of 1919-1922 had a single-cylinder engine above the rear wheel. (Below): From Gloucestershire came the well-enclosed Unibus scooter with 269cc 2-stroke engine and sprung wheels.

and inevitably many eager young men who had flown, driven or motorcycled during the war sought new excitement in racing. The classic Isle of Man TT was revived in 1920, bringing victory for overhead valves and multi-speeds in the 350cc (Junior) race by an AJS with four speeds hastily concocted from a two-speed countershaft box and two primary chains in P. & M. style. A two-stroke Levis won the new 250cc sub-class, and two side-valve Sunbeams won the Senior (500cc) race, sandwiching a side-valve Norton. But where performance counted, overhead valves were now well on the way and chain drive was an essential.

Other improvements were becoming manifest. Already largely emancipated from the bogeys of hillclimbing, punctures and breakdowns that dogged his predecessors, the postwar motorcyclist making a long trip no longer had to worry about petrol and oil supplies. New garages were being set up by enthusiastic ex-servicemen assisted by oil and fuel companies who arranged regular supplies and began to install manually operated petrol pumps to replace the old two-gallon can supply system. Even coin-in-the-slot 24-hour pumps were mooted, while home-produced benzole fuel, distilled from coal, came on to the market.

### Anticlimax

Roads were slowly being improved, electric lighting systems made night riding safer, and tires and plugs were now reliable. The hub gear was dead and belt drive dying, pedal starting gear had gone and the two or three speed countershaft gearbox with kickstart was becoming the norm; hub brakes were steadily ousting the rim type and the ancient stirrup, and controls were becoming more standardized, with clutch and ignition levers on the left of the handlebars, air and throttle levers to the right, and the hand gearchange on the offside of the tank.

Yet as 1920 advanced, an unexpected cloud gathered and darkened. Makers had mastered their production, material and labour problems, and motorcycles poured from the factories. Orders at last were being fulfilled, but new orders failed to come in. Price was the deterrent, for the cost of living had increased alarmingly, the bank rate had been raised in the spring, and the sinister 'inflation' that was making life in postwar Germany a nightmare hit Britain and other Allied countries to a lesser degree. Food, clothing and other commodities including cars and motorcycles became dearer. Models advertised and ordered at, say, £65 in 1919 cost more like £130 on delivery in 1920; orders were cancelled, and manufacturers began to withhold prices in their advertisements, or added a precautionary 'provisional' or 'current'.

Each week a new batch of price increases was announced, and incredibly as the year ran out makers found themselves faced with a slump. The fine new boom had fizzled out, trade fell off all round, workmen were paid off, and unemployment in the 'land fit for heroes to live in' topped a million barely two years after 'the war to end wars' had been won.

The more expensive car market was harder hit, and the figure of 278 600 British motorcycle registrations in 1920—well over twice the 1914 figure—still sounded impressive, especially with 21 285 motorcycles exported as well. Yet Britain then was the world's greatest producer of motorcycles, and given a stable world economy, that output could well have topped 300 000. Instead, as 1921 approached, a bewildered industry and public found they were expected to ride out a slump.

# WHEN BRITISH WAS BEST

"Today a motorcycle can be purchased for the price of a pedal cycle of 30 years ago."
Sir Harold Bowden, *The Motor Cycle*, 1926

That first postwar slump was short, sharp and salutary. It checked the excessive momentum of factories geared to ever-higher production regardless of markets which were dwindling because of high prices. Some of the smaller, under-capitalized enterprises regrettably died, as is the cruel law of the industrial jungle, while others turned to small economy machines to widen the gap between the motorcycle and the car.

The British authorities encouraged the trend with a new taxation system in 1921 whereby motorcycles weighing up to 200lb paid an annual road tax of 30s, whereas heavier machines paid £3, with an extra £1 for sidecars and three-wheelers. This brought an extra influx of small two-stroke proprietary engines, Villiers to the fore with their 269cc unit which was copied by several rivals. It also prolonged the existence of the outdated but cheap belt drive and inadequate brakes, but fortunately the new austerity was relatively brief.

Ford, Swift, Bean, Morris and other motor manufacturers pointed the way past the economic impasse by making spectacular price cuts; the motorcycle industry followed suit, and the high prices of 1920 began to tumble. More small manufacturing and sales concerns perished when stocks lost heavily in value, but gradually economic equilibrium was achieved, and with a weather eye open for further squalls, the industry could at last settle down to building sound motorcycles.

Without question, the 1920s was Britain's decade. It may seem incredible today, with Norton-Villiers a tottery 'bastion' of home defence against formidable foreign invaders from Japan, Italy and Germany, but in those days British-built motorcycles were very firmly the best in the world. Over 50 different makes, from big factories such as BSA, Triumph, Douglas, Ariel, Royal Enfield, Matchless and Norton, with hundreds of workers on the strength, to small local works employing perhaps two dozen, contributed a flood of up-to-date, well-built machines from small two-strokes to 1000cc twins, which reached all corners of the world and furthered the prestige behind the phrase 'British made'.

Once again racing was of profound importance. AJS's 350cc ohv model which had won the 1920 Junior TT, now equipped with a proper three-speed gearbox, scored a sensational double in 1921 by winning both the Junior and Senior races. In the latter event it defeated Indian, Norton and Sunbeam side-valve opposition, purely through better acceleration, lighter weight and superior steering, road-holding and braking, rather than sheer maximum speed, driving home a lesson to designers that benefitted the whole industry.

Opposition to the little AJS included an important newcomer, the 499cc Triumph Ricardo, with special cylinder head having four pushrod-operated inclined ohv in a pent-roof combustion chamber with central sparking plug. This unit was the work of fuel and engine 'breathing' expert Harry Ricardo, and the new 'Riccy' Triumph, as it was nicknamed, proved a popular sports model during the next few years. In the 1922 Senior TT it finished second, beaten only by a new version of the famous side-valve Sunbeam called the 'Longstroke' by reason of its 77 × 105mm cylinder dimensions. But this was the last TT win ever for a side-valve engine, and that same year Norton also tried pushrod ohv, Blackburne marketed a proprietary ohv unit which powered many British and Continental sports models, and even Sunbeam themselves experimented with a very fast pushrod sprint model.

### Overhead valves

The value of overhead valves for more efficient gas intake and combustion in an engine was no discovery exclusive to the British, of course. Grand Prix racing cars had employed them since 1907, and only inadequate materials and high cost had deterred motorcycle manufacturers from adopting the layout earlier. The Italians were quick to use them in the early 1920s, revealing a penchant for extremely potent little 175cc ohvs, while even stricken Germany had ohv machines by 1922, such as the well-built MFZ, the KG and the unusual watercooled Arco, with its carburettor in front of the engine and the exhaust emerging behind.

But international road racing was the forcing house, and it was there that British ohv machines—Douglases, Nortons, AJSs, etc—and British JAP and Blackburne engines largely ruled the roost. They did not win every race in every class, of course, Continental opposition being very spirited, but their overall predominance raised the average British ohv sports model above all others on world markets, right through into the 1930s.

Great British marques in the golden '20s included Norton, BSA and Sunbeam. (Above): James 'Pa' Norton with one of his famous machines. (Above right): A batch of new BSAs ready to board a special delivery train in 1923.
(Below): Seen in 1922 sidecar form, the side-valve 499cc Sunbeam – an impeccably finished, top-quality British machine with the famous 'Little Oil Bath' chain case.

Racing apart, 1922 ushered in a period of intense development in other directions. An exclusive new make, the Brough-Superior, had established itself. George Brough, himself the son of a motorcycle manufacturer, set out to create a virtual 'Rolls-Royce of motorcycles', as indeed its slogan became. Around twin-cylinder sv and ohv engines by JAP or MAG (by Motosacoche of Switzerland), he built superb, very fast top-quality machines distinguished by handsome plated petrol tanks straddling the top-tube 'saddle'-wise. The big and decidedly beautiful Brough became quite a cult, one of the most consistent devotees being Colonel T. E. Lawrence (Lawrence of Arabia), who in his time owned several of them.

The Zenith Gradua and Rudge Multi expanding-pulley variable transmissions—admirable compromises both—were supplemented and finally replaced by normal countershaft gearboxes and chain drive. P. & M. marketed a sporting version of their famous 'sloper', calling it the Panther. A young man named William Lyons and a partner produced a sleek aluminium sporting sidecar called the Swallow; 14 years later he was to launch the Jaguar car. Barr & Stroud marketed single and twin cylinder engines from 350 to 996cc with sleeve valves. Models of 350cc became very popular, Granville Bradshaw, creator of the hapless ABC, producing a new 'over the counter' oil-cooled Bradshaw ohv engine, while BSA rocked the market with a top quality all-chain side-valve '350' at less than £60.

### The lightweight boom

Legshields were introduced to counter the discomforts of wet weather motorcycling; pillion riding became popular, sensible riders now straddling the machine rather than riding 'side saddle' as in earlier days, and the old Woods cycle-type tire valve gave way to the Schrader 'press in' needle valve. Villiers now offered 150, 250 and 350cc two-stroke engines, all with their clever waterproof flywheel magneto which also provided electric lighting, and lightweight motorbikes poured off the lines, most of them having cheap, simple but outdated belt drive. Notable British examples were the open-framed 'ladies model' McKenzie, Excelsior, Sun, Levis and Rex Acme Minor. Wearying cyclists could buy the Cykleaid motorizing kit comprising a 133cc two-stroke engine, spring front forks, wheel and controls, all for £24 10s cash or on 'easy terms', while purists demanding two-strokes with more power and all-chain drive could buy the 225cc Royal Enfield or the 249cc Velocette.

The French took to lightweights with much enthusiasm, producing a bewildering choice of two-stroke 'clip ons' and mini-bikes, and a choice of Anzani, Aubier-Dunne, Train and other engines. Best bargains included a 75cc belt-drive Peugeot and a chain-drive Clément with tiny 35×45mm 43cc engine, single gear and a claimed fuel consumption of 400 miles per gallon! Both cost about the equivalent of £22 in French francs. The Germans too, seeking minimal-cost transport more than most at the time, welcomed the lightweight. Literally hundreds of small firms in Berlin, Nuremberg, Munich, Leipzig, Cologne and

L. Shelley

National Motor Museum

National Motor Museum

Enterprising Britishers; (Above): The famous 499cc 4-valve Triumph Ricardo of 1924. (Top left): An experimental 4-cylinder Royal Enfield built in 1920. (Far left): George Brough, the Nottingham manufacturer, with one of his renowned JAP-engined twins, an SS80 side-valve of 1922/23, and (bottom left) the first Brough Superior of all, the '90 bore' ohv JAP-engined Mk.1 of 1919, with handsome nickel-plated saddle tank.
(Left): A noted 'roadburner', the 490cc push-rod ohv Model 18 Norton in 1923 form.
(Below): A 1926 Excelsior with 350cc ohv Bradshaw oil-cooled engine.

National Motor Museum

elsewhere produced them while grappling with the repeated financial crises that afflicted them just after the war.

In 1921 a firm called Berliner Kleinmotoren AG reverted to 1886 Daimler basics by building a motorcycle with reinforced wooden frame called the Bekamo. It was not a success, but its two-stroke motor of charging pump type, designed by Hugo Ruppe, was quickly put on sale and was snapped up by innumerable 'backyard' firms eager to build motorcycles. Other proprietary engines were the DKW, also designed by Ruppe, and the Grade, while in 1924 Julius Loewy added a 142cc two-stroke which, he claimed, would run on any fuel including crude oil.

### The Depression

To list all the German marques involved would be futile. Who today knows of the Atlas, Kurier, Bodo, Hoco (another wood-framed model) or the Fix (by Lloyd of Bremen, subsequent makers of the Borgward car), the Apex, Ge-ma-hi, Hexe or Hess, and many, many more? Most represented the hopes of engineers who had husbanded enough Deutschmarks to buy a batch of parts, and erect and sell a few motorcycles, only to lose all in Germany's severe mid-1920s depression. Of over 300 German makes launched between 1922 and 1926, only BMW and Zündapp survive today, alongside the older-established NSU and DKW.

The Italians were just as keen as the rest on cheap road transport in those difficult times, but their government proved obdurate in taxing motorized bicycles and lightweight motorcycles as much as full-grown machines. This anomaly was not remedied until late in 1922, when the rush to build began and such makes as Gaia, Alato, Dardo, Ancora and Alfa (no relation to the car) appeared. Small Italian engines included the Piva, Fulgor and Rubinelli, but British Villiers, French Train, German DKW and Swiss Moser units also enjoyed brisk sales. Puch of Austria, Imholz and Forster of Switzerland, and the rare Meray from Hungary all swelled the flood of economy machines, while even the United States made a 'gas saver' in the Evans 'Power Cycle' with 119cc two-stroke engine. This sold well in Italy, while the German Stock concern of Berlin built a considerable number under licence.

Austerity designs are often ingenious but seldom very interesting. Where cost was secondary to efficiency or ideals, Continental engineers atoned with several exciting, exotic and sometimes eccentric machines. The Bayerische Motoren Werke of Munich, makers of successful six-cylinder aero-engines during the First World War, managed to weather the fierce economic storms of the early 1920s with a sophisticated motorcycle of outstanding potential. Beginning with a sparse 148cc powerbike called the Flink, they advanced by 1922 to a Douglas-like 500cc side-valve flat twin bearing the name Helios.

The engine was also sold to several other German makers, but meanwhile chief designer Dr Ing Max Friz drastically revised the Helios layout. He placed the flat-twin engine transversely in the frame, like the British ABC, then added a three-speed gearbox and car-type clutch, shaft final drive, and unusual but effective leaf-sprung trailing link front forks. Thus was born the BMW *motorrad,* which was a sensation at the 1923 Paris Salon. Assiduous development and the acid test of racing (BMWs won the gruelling motorcycling Targa Florio event in Sicily three years running from 1927 to 1929, besides innumerable other European races) brought the marque wide renown, and today, embodying the same design principles, it is world-famous.

### 'One-track Mauser'

More surprising was the machine built by Mauser armaments company between 1922 and 1927 to the design of Alfred Morgan of Nuremberg. Called the *Einspur-auto* or 'one-track car', it carried a body giving waist-high enclosure for two people in tandem, and had a windscreen, hood and bisected 'wheel' instead of handlebars. There were small support wheels on each side, recalling the pioneer Daimler *Einspur* and the American Biautogo of 1913. The engine was a watercooled 500cc side-valve single with the radiator in the nose of the body, cantilever rear springing featured, and a 90km/h (56mph) maximum speed was claimed. The Mauser was also built under licence in France as the Monotrace, which also means 'one track'.

Hailing from a more unexpected source, Denmark, was the very advanced Nimbus. This was patented in 1919 by P. A. Fisker of a famous Danish firm of electric motor and vacuum cleaner manufacturers in Copenhagen; it broadly followed the Belgian FN layout, with an aircooled in-line four-cylinder 750cc side-valve engine and shaft drive. Unorthodox, however, was its duplex cradle frame of welded flat steel members with transverse 'boxing', and the integral circular petrol tank giving great rigidity. The engine was mounted on a full-width steel platform, coil rear springing with swinging links was used, and an ancestor of the post-Second World War Earles-type leading link front fork was prescribed in the original patent.

By 1920, when the Nimbus went into small scale production, American-style forks were fitted, and this remarkable Danish machine was supplied to discerning customers until 1928, when pressure of other work stopped production. Indicative of its success as a design, however, was the fact that the Nimbus 'four' was revived in more modern ohc form in 1934, over 12000 in all being built up to 1959.

The neatness, silence and cleanliness of shaft drive as opposed to its cost would always beguile designers, but the rare French Lutèce combined both in 1921 with a 997cc in-line vertical twin aircooled engine-cum-transmission unit anticipating the Sunbeam S7 and S8 600cc models which appeared in the late 1940s. A rare British exponent was the GSD, which first allied a White & Poppe two-stroke engine with shaft drive in 1921. Two years later, coincidentally with BMW, the marque produced a transverse flat twin-engined motorcycle with four-speed gearbox and propeller shaft transmission. The engine was a Bradshaw, and there was an element of ABC inspiration, but unlike the BMW counterpart, this enterprise sadly fell on stony ground and expired. Ironically, the concern which popularized shaft drive, FN of Liège, replaced the system with chains in 1923 on the grounds that increasing engine power made the shaft transmission unreliable.

The two-wheeled car motif also attracted an American, C. A. Neracher of Syracuse, New York, who designed an unusual machine which he called the Neracar—a fortuitous pun on his own name and his design objective. It came close to car specification with its generous protection for the rider, enclosed working parts and low pressed-steel chassis. At the fore end this extended out and forward

National Motor Museum

EVERYDAY SC

A New Terror

Still another attempt at the one-wheeled motor-cycle. The inventor, E. J. Christie, of Marion, Iowa, U.S.A., hopes for speeds up to 250 miles an hour from the 14-foot model seen above. It is driven by chains from the 250-h.p. aerial motor below the axle. The two small interior wheels, for which there is a separate motor, act as gyroscopic balancers and rudders. At the left is a small model of a different type.

Everyday Science
& RADIO NEWS
FEB 1923
INCORPORATING "MODELS, RAILWAYS AND LOCOMOTIVES"
1/- nett
A NEW TERROR OF THE ROAD

Maurice Rickards

While enterprising Continental designers produced imaginative machines like the 1921 Moto-Guzzi with horizontal single-cylinder ohc engine (far left), the 1923 transverse flat-twin BMW with shaft drive (far right), and the Mauser 'Einspur-auto' 2-wheeled car (top left), American inventor E.J. Christie went to wildest extremes with his fantastic 250mph mono-wheel (above).

Radio Times Hulton

to form the horizontal front forks supporting hub-centre pivot steering of somewhat restricted lock

From a low-mounted, geared steering head handlebars sprouted inelegantly upwards above the protruding aircooled cylinder of the 211cc two-stroke engine. Unscrewing two nuts quickly removed a panel and laid bare 'the works', including friction drive from the flywheel to a countershaft carrying the final drive sprocket. A gear lever in a notched quadrant moved this wheel across the flywheel, giving five speeds.

Sheffield-Simplex Ltd, luxury car makers, built the Neracar in Britain under licence, with a 285cc two-stroke or larger Blackburne 350cc engines, and friction drive or normal Sturmey-Archer three-speed gearbox as options. De luxe versions with rear springing, a windscreen and bucket seat were also available. Once the rider had accustomed him- or herself to the geared-up steering, the Neracar proved a stable and reliable machine, but its sedate appearance was against it in a sporting era, and it died in 1926.

## American decline

Apart from rebels like Mr Neracher, however, the American motorcycling scene had reached stagnation. The transatlantic genius for quantity production brought a flood of cheap, dependable cars which offered far more comfortable transport than two wheels at little extra cost. Make after make dropped from the production 'tree'—Jefferson, Pirate, Peerless, Dayton, etc. during the First World War; Cyclone and Militaire by 1920; and Merkel by 1922, merged with Indian. Of all the fine husky twins of eight years earlier, only Indian, Harley-Davidson and Excelsior remained, and 'middle age' had made them all heavier and less agile.

## 'Yank bikes'

A considerable part of their production was for the American mobile police—the original 'speed cops'. Postwar sales in Europe were restricted by high prices, but the formidable strength and power of the 'Yank bikes' still made them desirable. The Germans got round the problem by building an imitation Indian, the Mabeco, in 600cc and 750cc forms; in Italy both Harleys and Indians won many races, while in Britain the historic 500-Miles Race at Brooklands in 1921 saw American motorcycles finish one-two-three, two Indians sandwiching a Harley-Davidson, with the best home machine, a 500cc side-valve Norton, in fourth place. Rubbing it in, a Harley turned the first over-100-mph motorcycle lap ever achieved on the Brooklands track in 1922, only to be beaten by a compatriot Indian a day later.

The American Excelsior concern, not to be confused with the British product from Tyseley, Birmingham, augmented their range of twins when, in 1917, they bought the manufacturing rights for the four-cylinder Henderson. Two years later William Henderson himself founded a new make, Ace, producing massive 1168 and 1229cc in-line aircooled 'fours' in competition with those bearing his name. He died in a road accident in 1922 but the Ace Company continued, one setting a new motorcycle world speed record at 129mph (208km/h) in 1923. Eventually financial troubles resulted in takeover by Indian four years later, the design reappearing as the Indian Four.

In Europe, at a time when every £1 in the price counted, when big manufacturers were saving costs by streamlining production methods and small ones, regrettably often, by skimping, another 'quality first' British design *à la* Sunbeam or Brough-Superior was welcome. This was the HRD, product of H. R. Davies who had won the historic Senior TT of 1922 on a Junior AJS.

For power he used the sturdy and popular 490cc ohv JAP engine, installing it in a well-designed duplex frame and topping it with a handsome saddle tank. Then he demonstrated that the new make was 'more than just a pretty face' by winning the 1925 Senior TT. Two years later another HRD won the Junior TT, and this fine 'bespoke' rather than 'ready-made' motorcycle was well launched. In 1929 manufacture was taken over by Phil Vincent, both the resultant spring frame Vincent-HRD and finally the Vincent became the high-performance classics which are so much revered today.

## The insatiable quest

By 1926 every major British make and most Continentals listed ohv models. P. & M. had even renounced all their side-valvers in favour of a neat new ohv unit for the popular Panther 'sloper'. Designed by Granville Bradshaw, it had its pushrods enclosed in a single tube, a fashion several others followed. Rudge-Whitworth finally scrapped their superannuated inlet-over-exhaust engine, replacing it with a thoroughly modern four overhead valve layout in conjunction with a four-speed gearbox. And in Germany, BMW fitted detachable ohv heads to their transverse flat-twin, as well as building a ferociously fast 750cc version.

Yet again racing proved its testbed value, when the insatiable quest for ever more performance turned many minds to overhead camshafts. After Peugeot's pre-1914 example several competition ohc engines appeared in the early 1920s, and then, in 1925, Velocette of Birmingham, former lightweight specialists, turned 'sporting' with a beautiful 348cc bevel-driven ohc model, the K. A year later a racing version won the Junior TT at record speed, and the classic 'cammy Velo' career, due to last into the 1950s, had begun.

Chater-Lea developed an attractive 350cc 'face cam' model designed by rider-engineer Dougal Marchant, and OEC of Portsmouth unveiled their 498cc Atlanta ohc engine with spiral bevel drive, both in 1925. On the Continent the appeal of fewer reciprocating parts was just as strong, particularly in Italy; in 1927, the marque Augusta of Turin outdid the many zestful ohv '175's with an ohc '125'. Higher up the capacity scale Bianchi of Milan employed gear-driven twin ohc on a formidable racing '350' called the *Freccia Celeste* or Blue Arrow; it caused much flutter in the British racing dovecot in the mid-1920s. And in 1927 Norton, too, switched from pushrod to camshaft valve operation, winning the Senior TT to show the world they had 'got it right' first time.

Diversity of purpose: (Left): The utility Neracar of 1921, an easy-to-ride utility machine with enclosed 211cc 2-stroke engine, 5-speed friction drive and hub-centre steering. (Right): The big Henderson '4' of the 1920s was ideal for long-distance American road work with its 1301cc aircooled in-line 4-cylinder engine. (Below): Art in metal, exemplified by the classic sporting 348cc overhead camshaft Velocette engine, introduced in 1925 and seen here in restored 1930 KSS form.

*National Motor Museum*

*Motor Cycle*

Radio Times Hulton

Motor Cycle

(Far left): A popular economy side-valve '250' for getting to work was the 249cc 'round tank' BSA. (Top left): Two young lady motor-cyclists set off for a rainy ride in 1925; their BSA machines are fitted with windscreens. (Bottom left): For use in desert and bush on a transworld tour in 1927, the owner of this 4-valve, 4-speed 499cc Rudge-Whitworth fitted out the sidecar to form a bed. (Right): A favourite sports '350', the AJS 'Big port' single of 1926. (Below): Harmony in line (and in its famous exhaust 'yowl'!)—the sleek 1927 Scott 'Flying Squirrel' twin 2-stroke.

National Motor Museum

National Motor Museum

Apart from the glamour of racing, the busy round of improvement and refinement continued apace. The year 1925 had seen two-port engines from Villiers, JAP and others, and whereas Rudge-Whitworth, New Hudson and one or two others were content to run the two pipes into one forward-mounted silencer (muffler), with a single tailpipe, others duplicated the pipes and silencers, one each side. The public liked them for their symmetry and 'busy' look, and although manufacturers rued the two-port system for the extra cost and weight it entailed, they valued it for its sales appeal.

The quiet family man, unmoved by such things, was not wholly neglected, for quite a choice of sturdy, slogging side-valve models was available, and gave yeoman service. Sales of all kinds of motorcycle were booming. In 1925 581 228 were registered in Britain alone, only 8928 fewer than cars. In 1926 the figure was 646 295 (695 634 cars), and in 1927 it rose to 690 675, while the car figure was 800 112, just over 10 000 more.

The price war continued. In 1924 BSA had produced a neat sv '250', commonly known as the 'Beeser round tank' or 'cocoa tin' model and a bestseller at 35 guineas. In 1926 Matchless and Raleigh produced similar models at 33 guineas and £36 respectively. Then Douglas dropped a bombshell with a smart 348cc flat-twin, the model EW, at £41 10s (acetylene generator, lamp and horn 30s extra!), getting a flood of orders. Triumph's bestselling 500cc side-valve Model P at £42 17s 6d was challenged by Ariel's 550cc sv at £45, while Rudge's four-valve four-speed ohv was a bargain at £46, which did not include lighting.

## Dream bikes

Jungle law prevailed, and old firms that could not modernize or stand the pace were dying off; Beardmore, Clyno, Connaught, Hobart, Lea-Francis, Bat, Martinsyde, McKenzie and Bradbury had all gone. Design was again tidied up. Internal expanding hub brakes at front and rear were fast displacing the rim brake, acetylene lighting receding before electrics, tires were growing fatter, straight tube centre-spring forks by Webb and Brampton were challenging the old and less comely curved-blade types.

The classic Scott twin two-stroke was offered in 1926 as the Flying Squirrel with an attractive new 'long tank' instead of the old 'bread bin', and for 1927 BSA launched a new 493cc ohv model with inclined engine and sump extending forward to form an oil reservoir. Lively, comfortable, reliable and extremely quiet, the 'Sloper' proved a great favourite with serious motorcyclists during the next few years. Another much-loved classic, the very sporting Model 90 Sunbeam, appeared in 1927; it had two-port pushrod ohv engine with all the Sunbeam workmanship, finish and beauty, and was one of the belles of the Olympia Show.

A *rara avis* at that 1927 Olympia Show was a one-off exercise by George Brough—an aircooled V4, with four separate 249cc cylinders paired at 60° on an aluminium crankcase. Side valves on the inside of the two banks activated by a single camshaft; ignition was by battery and coil, and final drive via a four-speed gearbox and chain. Finished to the customary Brough-Superior standards, with magnificent plated saddle tank and neat exhausts, its 'dream' quality was accentuated by the quoted price of £250.

The year 1928 was the 'saddle tank' year, when most manufacturers took up the fashion. Douglas, AJS and Sunbeam were among those who dallied, but the change became universal twelve months later. Concealing the frame top tubes, the saddle tank undoubtedly improved appearance, although its shape, like an inverted 'U', cost more to make than the old flat type. Strictly, some were pannier rather than saddle tanks, comprising two halves each side of the top tube, a technique already practised since 1916 in the United States, the gap being covered by a metal

1
2
3
4
5
6
7
8
9
10
11
12
B.S.A
BH 3661

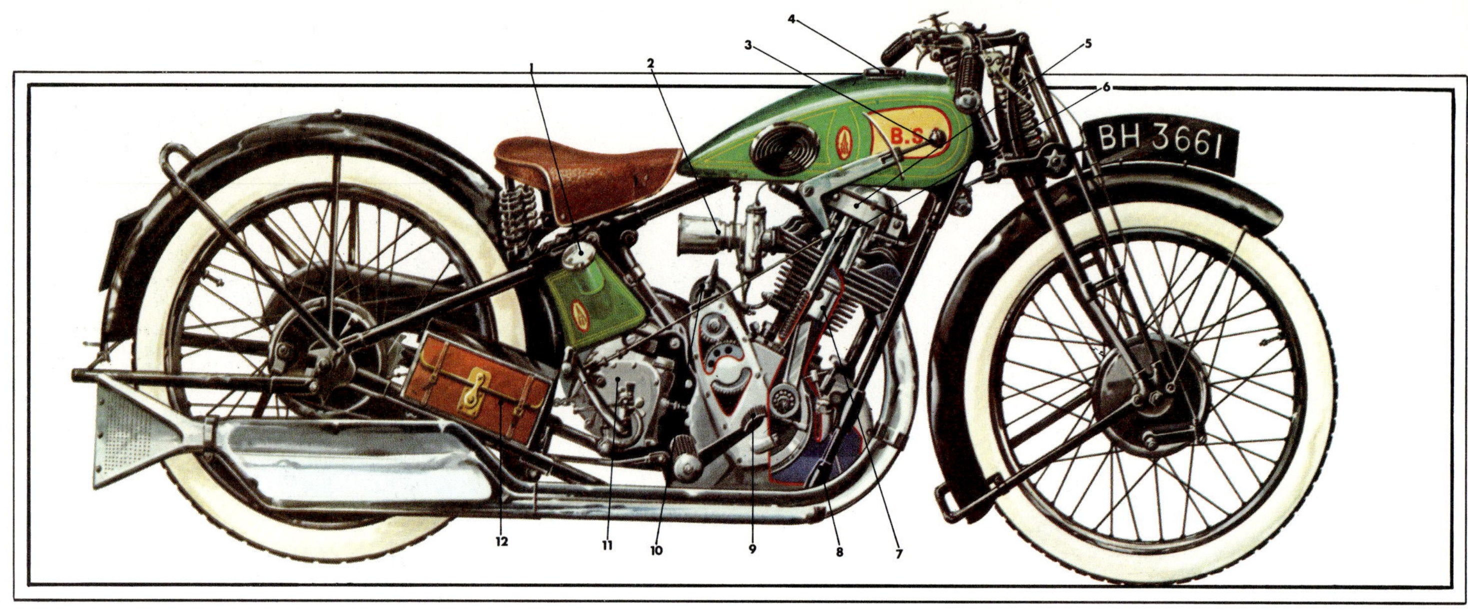

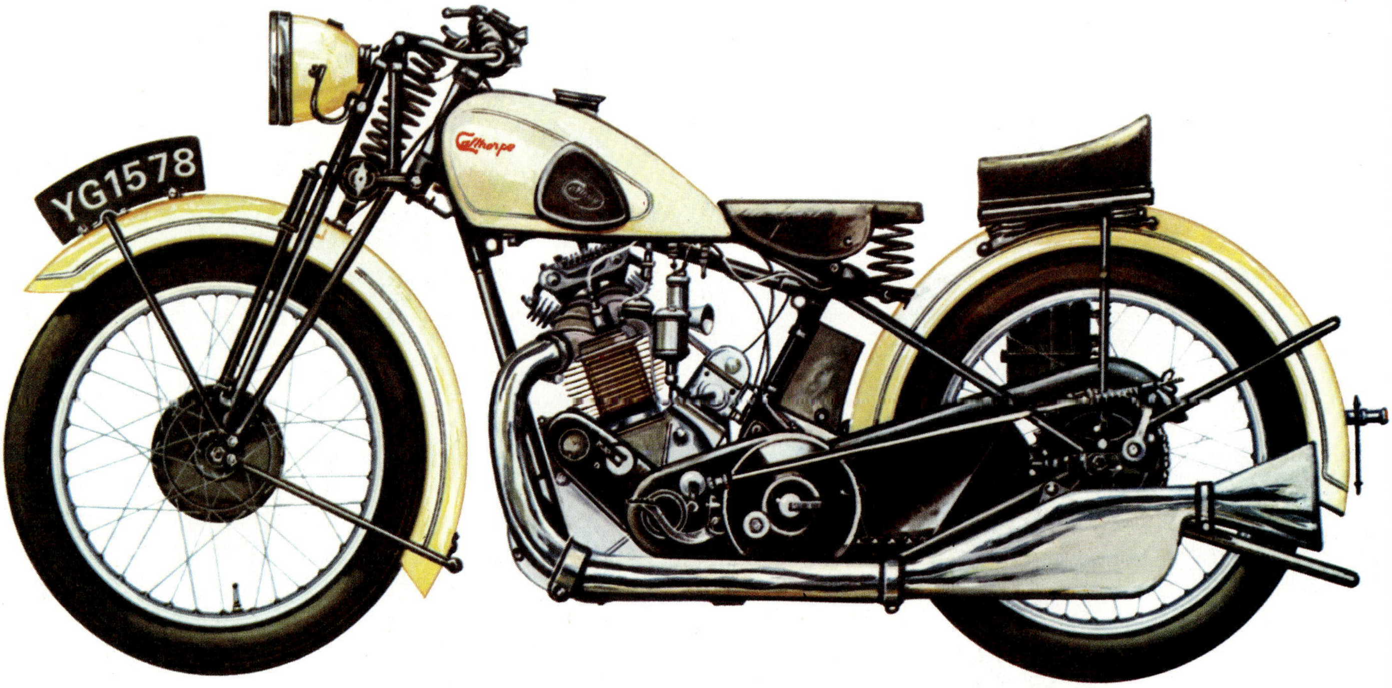
YG1578
Calthorpe

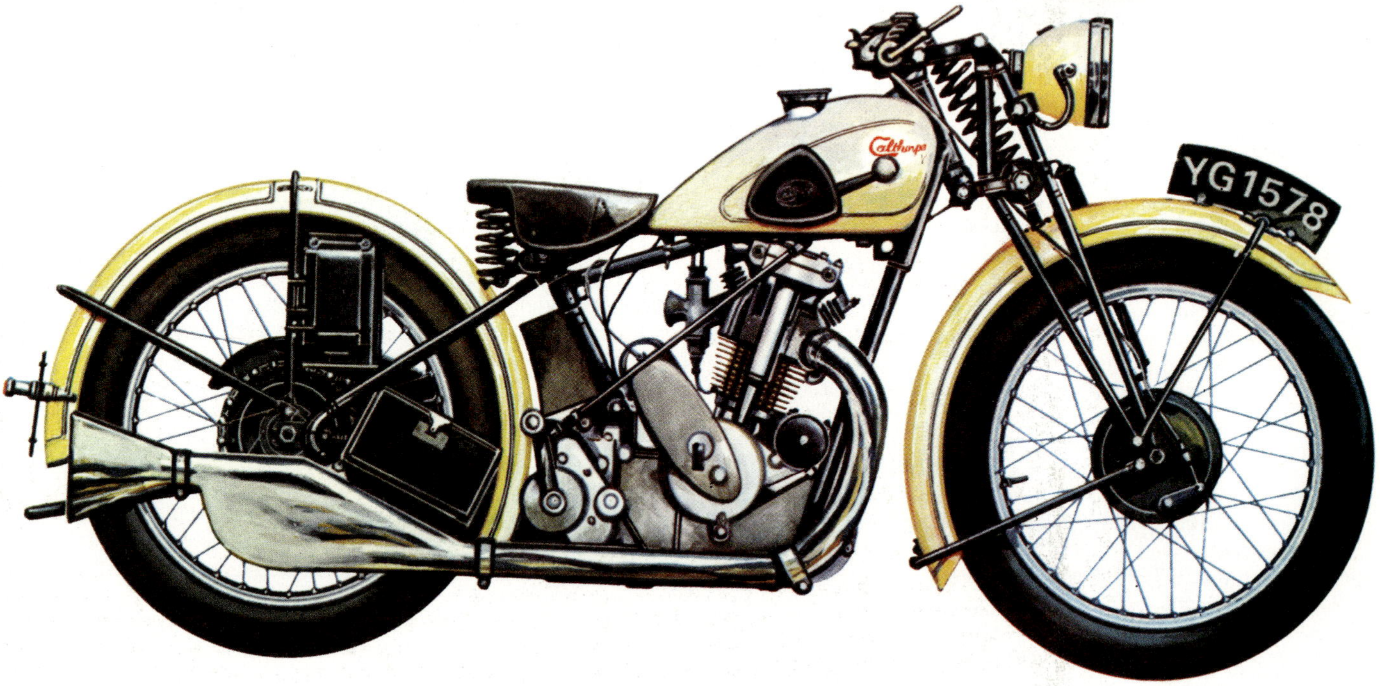
Calthorpe
YG1578

strip, either enamelled or plated. With such tanks, deeper saddles, pushrods disappearing within enclosing tubes, covered-in valve gear and bigger tires and brakes, the average motorcycle was beginning to lose its lissome vintage lines and acquiring a new, solid look.

### Chill wind

A slight chilling of the economic wind became apparent with a fresh outbreak of lightweights. Ariel cleverly preceded news of their new 250cc sv and ohv Colt models with a series of advertisements featuring the Ariel 'horse' trademark and hinting at an impending happy event. Matchless made a 250cc two-port ohv, New Imperial an under-200lb 350cc side valve; BSA stretched their already extensive range still further with a 174cc two-stroke costing all of £28 10s, while Coventry-Eagle introduced a clever 'baby' with pressed steel frame and forks in the Continental manner.

Panther also made a Villiers-engined lightweight, Zenith, famous for their twins, also stooped to a 172cc Villiers-powered model and an under-200lb side-valve '300', and Rudge-Whitworth added 250cc JAP-engined 'tiddlers' to their range of 'roadburners'. Perhaps most typical of the cheap, colourful 'styled' models of that era was the 'Ivory' Calthorpe made by the long-established Birmingham firm. By dint of careful tooling, concentration in Ford Model T style on one model only, and stringent pricing, they were able to offer an attractive two-port '350' with enclosed ohv at a challenging £47 (electric lighting extra). Performance was 'average', but with its neat lines and all-white saddle tank and mudguards (fenders) this machine sold well.

The Olympia Show 'surprise' was now an eagerly awaited annual event, and 1928 brought not one but several! The futuristic Ascot-Pullin, lineal descendant of the Pullin-Groom of 1921-25, was the brainchild of Cyril Pullin, former racing motorcyclist, 1914 Senior TT winner, and a keen designer with radical ideas. Its 500cc ohv engine was mounted horizontally like the Guzzi, with unit construction gearbox; the frame and forks were of pressed steel, hydraulically operated front and rear brakes were fitted, and the enclosed kickstarter was coupled with the valve lifter. Rider luxuries included built-in legshields, a retractable windscreen with wiper and an instrument panel integral with the handlebars. A two-tone cellulose finish was featured, and a hydraulic-braked, pressed-steel sidecar in complement cost £17.

### British 'fours'

Pullin's efforts were somewhat overshadowed at Olympia that year by no fewer than three new British 'fours'! George Brough sprang another surprise with a 900cc side-valve in-line 'four', replacing his V4 of 1927. The engine was built for Brough by Motosacoche of Geneva, and the bicycle parts included a Draper spring frame. With twin headlights, Brough's 'Castle' forks of Harley-Davidson inspiration, deeply valanced mudguards (fenders) and large pannier toolboxes, this was a magnificently massive 'gimmick' exhibit. A retail price of £200 effectively prevented a waiting list of customers, although that inveterate Brough enthusiast Colonel T. E. Lawrence ordered one.

### Wall Street crash

Two lesser known British makers, McEvoy of Derby and AJW of Exeter, contributed the other 'fours'. The former showed the 'Cyclone' in neat 594cc in-line aircooled form; the latter offered the 'Super-Four', a radical machine with car-type channel-section chassis and low-pivot steering, and a 985cc in-line four-cylinder sv watercooled engine, actually a British Anzani car unit neatly adapted to motorcycle confines. The fuel tank was out of sight below the saddle, a dummy in the usual place merging with most attractive closed 'bodywork' set off by straight-swept exhausts.

Alas, the late 1920s was not an opportune time to launch inevitably expensive, unconventional projects, and the Ascot-Pullin flat-single and the Brough, McEvoy and AJW in-line 'fours' had all departed by the close of the decade. The motorcycle industry had, indeed, to draw in its horns in 1929, that black year which brought the Wall Street crash in October, precipitating a world-wide depression lasting for over four years, with countless company failures and world-wide unemployment in train.

Although costing around £50 more, the cheap 'baby' car as exemplified by the Austin Seven, Morris Minor or Triumph Super Seven in Britain was making serious inroads into the

(Top left): The 1928 493cc BSA 'sloper'. 1: Reserve oil tank. 2: Carburettor. 3: Gear lever control. 4: Petrol cap. 5: Valve gear. 6: Push rods. 7: Piston and connecting rod. 8: Cradle frame. 9: Rear brake pedal. 10: Magneto. 11: Gear box. 12: Tool box. (Below left): Near and off-side views of the 1930 350cc 'Ivory' Calthorpe with inclined ohv engine. (Right): The 500cc Ascot-Pullin with pressed steel frame and forks, horizontal engine, hydraulic brakes and lavish weather protection.

National Motor Museum

luxury motorcycle and sidecar outfit trades. Four people within the confines of a small box-like saloon were nonetheless more comfortable in the average British weather than two or three on a combination, exposed to wind, wet and cold. Moreover, the false security of the 'never never' or 'glad and sorry' easy payments system, as popular then as now, weighed against the motorcycle by making the extra cost look less formidable. For makers, money was becoming scarcer, sales meant a harder fight, and they had carefully to balance their production costs against those necessary for keeping up with current fashion and luring the buyer.

The two major innovations on the 1930 models shown at Olympia late in 1929 were inclined engines and chromium plating. The inclined engine, long used by Panther and Cotton, and more recently by BSA, was aesthetically pleasing and helped to lower machine height slightly. Chromium plating, introduced on American cars in 1928, was a boon, removing the tedious 30 years' chore of polishing nickel plate. Chromium, a bright, hard, non-tarnishing finish, was electro-deposited upon a nickel-plated base, which was itself on a copperplate base if the job was done properly. It soon became a 'must' on exhaust pipes, controls, fittings and petrol tanks, looking very effective in conjunction with coloured cellulose panels.

Seasonal tidying up brought the first 'clean' handlebars by Triumph, with control fulcrums and cable guides brazed in place instead of being clipped on. Austerity told on cheap lightweights with a tendency towards black-painted silencers (mufflers) and handlebars, and pressed steel forks. The dry sump lubrication system was adopted by several makes. In the eyes of worshippers, Norton demeaned themselves by following fashion and 'going two-port' and 'chrome-tanked' on two models, while New Imperial took much trouble producing a 'two-port' side-valve by discharging the exhaust into a cast aluminium finned chamber which carried twin exhaust pipes.

A new, short-lived British make was the Berwick, with Villiers engine turned askew to take shaft drive, while another unusual newcomer, ostensibly English, was the Newmount. Its frame and forks were made from slim H-section forged steel members, and the Continental-looking two-stroke engine with outside flywheel betrayed its origin—it was a German Zündapp in special import guise!

BSA had a forged steel 'backbone' member in place of the normal top tubes between steering head and saddle. Coventry-Eagle, who had made a side-valve 'Flying Eight' big twin for several years, tried to 'do a Brough' with a rakish-looking 998cc ohv JAP-motored Model 160. It cost £120 to Brough's equivalent at over £150, but like the Rolls-Royce car, the Brough-Superior motorcycle could be emulated but not equalled. George Brough's big Show attraction that year was the conventional 680cc twin ohv Black Alpine with black and gold finish, so it fell this time to the long-established London firm of Matchless to provide the one real Olympia 'surprise'.

This was the 'Silver Arrow', a 400cc side-valve 'monobloc' twin with the cylinders cast in one block at the narrow angle of 26°, and a double-coil spring frame. It was no 'speed iron' but a smooth, comfortable touring machine, heavy at 336lb and with modest performance eloquent, perhaps, of the subdued key on which the vigorous vintage decade of motorcycle development ended. From it, however, was to spring the four-cylinder Matchless 'Silver Hawk' which, with the equally sensational Ariel 'Square Four', took Britain on the crest of the wave out of the boisterous 1920s into the stormy 1930s.

National Motor Museum

Motor Cycle

**The 1928 594cc 4-cylinder McEvoy 'Cyclone' (above); 1928 998cc vee-twin ohv Coventry Eagle-JAP (below); and the 1930 400cc monobloc twin Matchless 'Silver Arrow' (in oval).**

Maurice Rickards

# CONTINENTAL CHALLENGE

"Just ask any foreign country what it would give to swop motorcycle industries with us . . ."
'Ixion', *The Motor Cycle,* 1932

It is a remarkable testimony to the buoyancy of the world motorcycle industry in the 1930s that, despite a deep trade depression in the first half of the decade, and world-shaking political upsets in the second, it should have produced so stimulating a variety of designs. When 'economize' was the dismal watchword in most countries, and purchase price and running costs were of desperate importance to motorcycle sales, there was inevitably a plethora of cheap machines of sound but uninteresting design. Yet these were offset by brilliant new 'multis' and lively sports models from Britain and the Continent of Europe.

It seems amazing in retrospect that when every order had to be fought for, an industry with its back to the wall could have sustained so many manufacturers. In Britain over 40 different makes contested world sales in 1931, while despite smaller markets, French, German and Italian marques each numbered well over a score. In every factory, production costs were of extreme importance and all design innovations demanded the most careful consideration lest the delicate balance between profit and loss be upset. That it frequently was is evidenced by the massive sales through main dealers at around Motorcycle Show time of brand new, unsold models of the previous year at attractive reductions, and this symptom of over-production and poor sales persisted into the middle of the decade.

In such a chilly economic climate the appearance of not one, but *two* new and very advanced British four-cylinder designs was indeed sensational. The rival makers, Matchless and Ariel, were both major concerns able up to a point to 'live off their own fat' in lean times, but they would probably have held back their expensive new 'fours' could they have foreseen the extent of the depression. Both designs were admirably compact in contrast with previous 'fours' such as the American in-line units and the abortive V4 Brough Superior of 1928.

The Matchless, called the 'Silver Hawk', was announced first, its engine recalling the earlier Lancia Lambda car unit in having an 18° narrow-angle monobloc form. In fact it was virtually the Matchless 'Silver Arrow' twin of the previous year doubled up, but with smaller cylinders at an even tighter angle, and a combined capacity of 593cc. It was aircooled, and the detachable head had an overhead camshaft driven by shaft and bevels, with a skew drive for a Lucas coil ignition/distributor unit. The three-bearing crankshaft was athwart the frame, driving a primary chain to a separate four-speed gearbox and chain final drive, and the 'Silver Hawk's other novelty was its rear suspension by twin coil springs and a triangulated rear section pivoting behind the gearbox.

### Ariel's 'Square Four'

Ariel also favoured the 'square' formation for its compactness and even cooling, but instead of a single crankshaft and angled cylinders, designer Edward Turner prescribed four vertical cylinders in an aircooled monobloc casting and parallel crankshafts geared together, with a chain-driven single overhead camshaft operating two valves per cylinder, and the carburettor in front of the engine. In effect the action was that of two vertical twins turning in opposite directions, giving exceptionally smooth torque, and the Ariel 'Square Four', though lacking the spring frame of the Matchless, compensated by being lighter and livelier.

Both were relatively expensive—£75 for the 'Silver Hawk' and £75 10s for the 'Square Four'—but both gave superbly smooth and effortless performance in solo or sidecar form with a flexibility and silence completely unknown at that time of 'thumping' singles. However, their fates differed widely: the Matchless lasted a mere five years with a

Motor Cycle

Above: The year 1931 saw the cult of the inclined engine taken to excess by Ariel on their 499 cc single-cylinder Model SG31 with four-speed gearbox. Despite its slinky appearance and lower centre of gravity, it was dropped by 1933.

Below: One of two sensational new models seen at the 1930 Olympia Motorcycle Show was the 597 cc Matchless 'Silver Hawk' with four cylinders in a narrow-angle monobloc vee, shaft-driven overhead camshaft, and a spring frame. It cost £75 and was produced up to 1935.

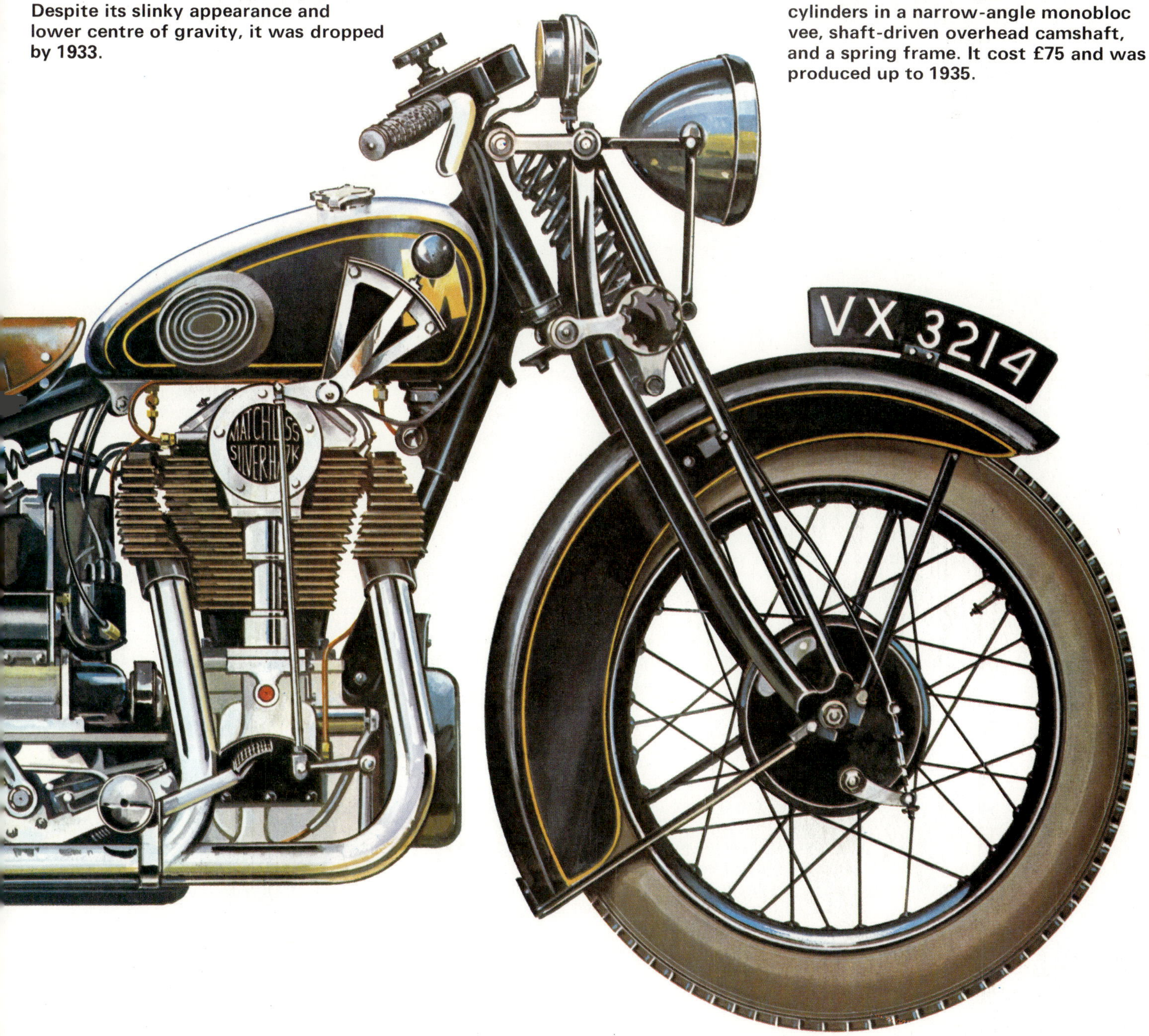

**Olympia's other sensation in 1930 was the 497cc Ariel 'Square Four', with chain-driven overhead camshaft, two geared crankshafts and roller bearing big ends. So neat and compact was the power unit that it fitted into the frame of a normal single-cylinder Ariel and weighed little more.**

production of only just over 500, whereas the Ariel's career was spread over 28 years, during which it grew, first to 600cc, then to 1000cc, and the overhead camshaft gave way to quieter pushrod valve operation, and a spring frame was developed.

These exciting 'fours' were naturally the 'plums' of the 1931 season, overshadowing three new and rakish but vibratory 500cc overhead valve vee-twins – the Montgomery 'Greyhound', James 'Flying Ace' and Brough Superior 'Overhead 500'. The Ariel company had two strings to their 'surprise' bow, with a new four-valve '500' which took the inclined engine theme to extremes, the cylinder being at 30° from horizontal. It discharged into an expansion chamber and twin exhaust pipes, the result being a commendably quiet single. With competition intensifying for dwindling sales, defensive measures were taken by Rudge-Whitworth who marketed their fine four-valve engines as 'Python' proprietary units in contention with JAP, Sturmey-Archer, Blackburne and MAG, while Velocette bowed to the inevitable and produced a cheaper ohc model, the KTP, with coil ignition and the fashionable twin exhaust ports. Humber, a rival marque with a two-wheeler history going back to the dawn of the century, withdrew altogether from the race, their new proprietors, the Rootes group, deciding to concentrate on car manufacture.

The cost factor dictated that most design improvements be minor, some like the upswept exhaust pipe craze and chromed petrol tanks merely pandering to fashion, whereas others had more significance, none more so than the foot gearchange. Ever since variable gears were introduced in about 1911, the rider had been obliged to remove one hand from the handlebars whenever he wished to change gear with the lever on the right hand side of the tank. Crafty dispatch riders in the First World War had found that, by bending down the gearbox-mounted lever on the three-speed WD Triumph, they could change gear with a deft 'hook' of the foot, thereby keeping both hands on the bars to cope with shell-blasted French and Flemish roads.

As usual, it was racing which finally forced the issue. In 1928 H. J. Willis of the Velocette concern invented a positive-stop footchange which bolted on to the three-speed gearbox of their 350cc ohc racing machines. The device assisted them to a dramatic 1-2 victory in the 1928 Junior TT race, saving them an estimated 30 seconds on each $37\frac{1}{2}$-mile lap of the Isle of Man circuit. It quickly became the accepted racing wear, and by 1932 the first footchanges were being offered on production sporting models. By 1936 handchange was practically obsolete.

### Tidying it up

The general untidiness of the single-cylinder motorcycle, with its aircooled engine and separate gearbox, prompted a praiseworthy effort by New Hudson on their 1931 models. A one-piece curved metal shield covered the crankcase, magneto, dynamo, gearbox, clutch and primary drive, leaving no nooks and crannies to harbour dirt. The shields were held in place by broad-headed screws easily turned by screwdriver or a coin, and Triumph obviously thought it a good idea, producing their own variation on the theme four weeks later! Neither lasted long in a market where an important youthful percentage of customers were averse to anything considered 'sissy' or 'non-sporting'. Triumph dropped theirs 12 months later, while in 1933 New Hudson gave up the precarious motorcycle trade altogether to take up manufacture of Girling car brakes.

Three important makers, Rudge-Whitworth, Scott and BSA, elected to stay away from the 1931 Olympia Motorcycle Show on economy grounds, while AJS was another lamented absentee. The old-established Wolverhampton firm of A. J. Stevens had, in fact, hit dire financial trouble and was taken over by Matchless of Woolwich, London. A final fling by AJS while still independent had been an unusual 496cc 50° sv transverse vee-twin, but Matchless quickly disposed of this design and its machine tools to a Japanese concern which employed the engine in a commercial vehicle into the 1950s.

At the somewhat depleted Show, Brough Superior again supplied the 'stunt' exhibit, an Austin Seven four-cylinder engined luxury bike intended for sidecar work only, having shaft drive passing between twin rear wheels. The price, with sidecar, was £188, and ten were built. Down at the realistic end of the price scale came a spate of what were nicknamed 'Snowden' models, after Viscount Snowden, the Chancellor of the Exchequer in the Labour government of the time. To encourage economy, he had halved the 30-shilling road tax applicable to all motorcycles weighing under 224 lb (100 kg) to 15 shillings for those under 150cc engine capacity. Villiers of Wolverhampton, the famous engine makers, were major beneficiaries as orders poured in for their simple, reliable little

**Above: Cheap and nippy. The New Imperial 'Unit Minor' introduced in 1932. Its 150cc inclined engine had overhead valves, and was built in unit with the three-speed gearbox; pressed steel forks were employed, and legshields, electric lighting and horn were included in the attractive price.**

**Below: Clean and decent. New Hudson motorcycles of 1931–33, as epitomized by this 500cc ohv model were fitted with a neat one-piece metal shield covering the crankcase of the engine and the four-speed Moss gearbox.**

147cc two-stroke units with flywheel magneto ignition.

Sun, Excelsior, Wolf, Radco, Dot, Rex Acme and Gloria (a short-lived offshoot of Triumph) all built Villiers-powered 'Snowden babies' at prices as low as £16 16s (minus lighting), while in 1932 New Imperial produced the 'Unit Minor', a very successful ohv '150' with unit construction of engine and gearbox, and pressed steel forks, which raised their sales by 48 per cent in the next 12 months. That same year Villiers went even smaller with a 98cc engine and two-speed gear in unit, the cheapest user being Excelsior at a mere £14 14s. While these tiny conveyances were extremely cheap to run, their power reserves were limited, and critics called them 'flat country bikes'.

### Hard times

The economic blizzard blew on and unemployment rose. The motorcycle trade, largely dependent on sales among weekly wage earners, was hard hit and the British industry, though exporting machines to some 70 countries, decided to cancel the 1932 Olympia Show. Quality makers produced 'cheap lines'; the lordly Panther 500 and 600cc 'slopers' were supplemented by new 250 and 350cc Red Panthers having engines only slightly inclined in normal frames, and selling at highly competitive prices under the sole distributorship of the big London dealers, Pride & Clarke. Rudge also produced a '250', with four valves, and Matchless contrived to build an under-224 lb, 30-shilling tax two-port 'Light 500' at only £35.

On the Continent things were tougher still. The German motorcycle makers decided they could not afford to support the combined Berlin car and motorcycle show in 1931, and pulled out. All motorcycles of under 200cc were exempted from tax, the result being an influx of 'featherweights' by DKW, Stock, Victoria, Zündapp, NSU, etc. Even BMW made a 198cc single, retaining their famous shaft drive, while NSU enjoyed brisk sales of a 63cc 'clip on' motor, fixed above the forks

**Right: A rare import into Britain from Germany in 1931 was the Nuremberg-built Ardie with British 490cc pushrod ohv JAP engine and Burman three-speed gearbox. With polished frame and chromed petrol tank, the machine was aptly named 'Silver Eagle'.**
**Below: The FN concern of Belgium, famous in earlier days for their shaft-driven four-cylinder machines, produced some lively singles in the 1930s, including this unusual 500cc ohv sports model, the M86 SP of 1934, advanced in having unit engine/gearbox construction and hairpin valve springs.**
**Opposite: A perfect summer setting for motorcycling as depicted by BSA on their 1935 catalogue. The leading machine is a 250cc ohv model, while behind is a sporting 'Blue Star'.**

*Motor Cycle*

*Cyril Posthumus*

of an ordinary cycle to drive the front wheel by chain in the famous (or infamous) pre-1900 Werner style.

In Germany's very fluid commercial situation at that time, old names died and new ones were born. D-Rad were taken over by NSU, the enterprising 1000cc transverse twin Windhoff disappeared, and the Opel car concern abandoned their second 'dabble' in the two-wheeler market; this arose in 1928 when they acquired the Elite works in Saxony and essayed production of an eccentric Dural-framed Neumann-Neander design, the very ugliness of which surely helped to kill it off. Yet in Tübingen a new make, Maico, quietly started up, building 98cc and 125cc lightweights with Sachs and Ilo engines and being destined for post-war fame in international motocross contests, while a new Aachen-built machine rejoicing in the name of BAM was a Belgian FN built under licence.

The marque Ardie of Nuremberg even tried importing their wares into Britain, but their clever 'Silver Eagle' model with 500cc JAP motor, Burman gearbox, Duralumin cradle frame, pressed steel forks and ugly silencers was unattractive in comparison with British machines—an important point with fickle customers when the price was over £60. From Prague, Czechoslovakia, came a 500cc ohv motorcycle called the Jawa, product of a small-arms factory headed by Ing. F. Janecek under licence to the German Wanderer marque—hence the name Jawa, combining the two leading letters of the progenitors. The English engineer George Patchett, formerly with Brough Superior and McEvoy, became chief Jawa designer in the 1930s, and besides building racing machines which carried their name abroad, they turned out increasing numbers of sound 'bread and butter' two- and four-strokes; today, allied with CZ, Jawa are the major Czech motorcycle producers.

B·S·A Motor Cycling Annual
BSA
AOF 494
Issued by B.S.A. Cycles Ltd., Birmingham 11.

Vintage Motor Cycle Club

Motor Cycle

**Left: Typifying the prewar sporting British motorcycle was the 1932–33 Royal Enfield 'Bullet', its inclined ohv single-cylinder engined sectioned here to show the internals. Built as a 250, 350 or 500, it had a four-speed gearbox with foot gearchange, and the popular upswept twin exhaust pipes. Engine oil was carried in a forward extension of the crankcase, and the 500cc model had a four-valve engine.**
**Above: A big seller in the highly competitive small four-stroke market was the 250cc ohv P & M 'Red Panther', which cost £29.17.6 'all-on' in 1933, marketed and distributed by one concern, Pride & Clarke of London.**
**Below, left: A popular utilitarian mount with commendable enclosure of working parts and excellent all-weather protection was the Francis-Barnett 'Cruiser' with 249cc two-stroke Villiers engine, introduced for 1933. The shielding could be removed without tools for maintenance in 90 seconds.**

## Russian motorcycles

With the launching of its first Five Year Plan in 1928, Soviet Russia committed itself to extensive land mechanization and the creation of large-scale vehicle industries. These included motorcycles, and early fruits were the Krasnyj-Oktabr, a utilitarian 300cc two-stroke built at Leningrad, and the Isch, which was a massive 1200cc side-valve twin with the engine set transversely and driving by shaft. It had Indian-style leaf fork springing and a pressed steel frame, and was built with heavy police duty chiefly in mind. Another early Russian make was the 600cc sv Tiz-Am, built at Kharkov, and all such motorcycles were entirely for domestic use, mostly by officials, the Soviet having no interest in exports in those days.

In Italy the small, high-revving 175cc ohv four-stroke was still extremely popular, over 20 factories turning them out. They were light on fuel yet lively enough to please the Latin temperament. Petrol (gasoline) in Italy was expensive, and one maker, Mariana, built a '500' to run on naphtha, which cost a quarter the price of *benzina,* although supplies were erratic and it was inefficient for starting. A special priming petrol tank solved that, but two carburettors were also needed. A more significant development was launched in Italy when a clever one-off engine design, the transverse in-line four-cylinder OPRA designed by Ing. Remor, was taken over by an aeronautical engine research company in Rome called CNA. The 500cc engine they produced in 1934, with twin ohc and roller-bearing crankshaft, went into a water-cooled racing motorcycle called the Rondine (or Swallow) with sprung rear wheel. Following some encouraging success, the four-cylinder Rondine design was taken over by Gilera, who scored countless race wins with it, rivalled late in their career by the similar, Remor-designed MV-Agusta. From the basic format of these superb, precision-built Italian multis are descended all modern four-cylinder road machines such as the Honda, Kawasaki, Suzuki and Benelli.

In the austere early 1930s, France's frugal *vélomoteurs* with microscopic engines and skimpy frames came into their own. There were literally dozens of different makes which, with seemingly nil maintenance, would carry 200-lb riders without protest on daily journeys to and from work. Larger French motorcycles were more technically adventurous than their average British counterparts, though competing in a smaller market. Marques such as Train, Motoconfort, Motobécane and Chaise were no strangers to four in-line cylinders and shaft drive, while fan-cooling, aluminium cylinders with steel liners and engine/gearbox unit construction were frequently encountered.

The defensive 'group' complex was already beginning, with Olympic, Labor, Armor, Thomann and Diamant all operating under the Alcyon umbrella, and all similar in design, while Terrot, the largest French motorcycle maker, and Magnat-Debon were in combine. Moreover the distinguished Koehler-Escoffier marque, who produced particularly inspiring 1000cc ohc twin-cylinder high-performance machines of Brough class, had been taken over by Monet-Goyon, who promptly augmented the K-E range with some unexciting

German quality. The Munich-built BMW with its classic transverse flat-twin engine and shaft drive was a fine but expensive Continental prestige machine, ideal for long-distance use as a solo or sidecar outfit. This is the 1935 750cc side-valve R12, with twin carburettors and one of the world's first tubular telescopic front forks.

Cyril Posthumus

but more profitable 'bread and butter' two-strokes.

The slump also hit America's already much reduced motorcycle industry. In 1931 manufacture of both the Excelsior vee-twins (sold in Europe under the name American X) and of the big Henderson in-line fours was stopped. Foreseeing a worsening of the depression, the Chicago-based company building both pulled out before sustaining heavy losses, and reverted to cycle making. Substantial American police orders probably saved the expensive Indian Four from a similar fate, while Indian continued building their massive vee-twins, as did Harley-Davidson, both designs little changed basically since the early 1920s.

### More British '150's

Back in Britain, Viscount Snowden's 'gift' snowballed still further in 1933, bringing neat little ohv '150's from Triumph and Excelsior, while Royal Enfield of Redditch introduced a smart little 148cc two-stroke called the 'Cycar', fully enclosed by metal panels and really 'hoseable'. Even Douglas, faithful to the flat twin since 1907, offered an enclosed '150' with two-stroke engine laid horizontally. Alas, the old Bristol firm was in deep financial trouble, and only the acquisition of a majority shareholding by the retired founder, William Douglas, rescued it from extinction.

Several other long-established names could not escape that fate, however. Ivy, Dot, New Henley, Radco, NUT, Royal Ruby and Rex-Acme, all well known in their time, dropped from the maker's lists, as did the Zündapp-based Newmount. AKD (Abingdon King Dick) went back to making spanners and other tools, and Raleigh to bicycles and an unsuccessful three-wheeler. But all was not gloom. Velocette augmented a distinguished range with a clever high-camshaft '250', the MOV, less expensive than their classic ohc models but pleasingly lively. And OK-Supreme launched a tentative new, higher-quality marque, albeit short-lived, in the Majestic, powered by an 'Ajax' engine made by the famous Stevens brothers, now free from AJS commitments.

By the summer of 1933 the world slump was lifting, and design enterprise at last could look beyond the inhibiting cost factor. New models poured forth in time for the Olympia Show in November, Triumph to the forefront with an important 649cc vertical (or 'parallel') aircooled twin designed by Val Page. It had a 360° crankshaft, i.e. with crankpins in line and the two pistons 'in step', rising and falling together, thereby providing even firing impulses at some cost in balance. It also had primary drive by double helical gears instead of a chain (a system 'borrowed' from the unit-construction New Imperials) and although the Triumph 650 proved heavy and expensive, it was nevertheless the harbinger of the coming 'vertical twin' revolution.

The Triumph was but one of the Show 'surprises'; BSA, Douglas and OEC contributed more. Having merged with the Daimler car concern in 1931, BSA sought to adapt their famous 'Fluid Flywheel' hydraulic transmission to a motorcycle. A 499cc single-cylinder ohv engine was harnessed to a miniature fluid flywheel and Wilson preselector gearbox, gears being preselected by a lever on the handlebars and engaged by dabbing a pedal. In truth, this apparent advantage compared poorly with the positive-stop footchange, while the unsympathetic 'single cylinder' torque and the weight and cost of the transmission made the project unpractical.

If, in fact, the 'Fluid Flywheel' BSA was purely a Show gimmick, the crowds it attracted had other novelties to keep them on the stand. These included a new 498cc ohv vee-

Cyril Posthumus

Douglas of Bristol made a gallant effort with the 500cc side-valve 'Endeavour' of 1935, in which their classic flat-twin engine was set transversely, BMW fashion, and drove the rear wheel through a four-speed gearbox and a propeller shaft. It was not a success, but the engine layout was revived by Douglas after the war.

twin for which BSA had received orders both from the Army and the police, for Britain's new 'speed cops', and also a compact little 149cc ohv 'Snowden' lightweight. Douglas's surprise was an enterprising variation on their flat-twin theme, the 500cc engine with aluminium barrels being turned round 90° to fit transversely in a wide cradle frame, with shaft drive to complete the BMW image. Unobtrusive spring steel bumper bars protected the cylinder heads, and the 'Endeavour', as it was called, was an attractive design that deserved a better fate than that suffered by so many other 'dream bikes'. But £72 10s was a considerable sum in those £5 a week days, and even when reduced to £59 10s sales were few, only about 50 being produced.

Motor Cycle

Above: Big American. The imposing 1229cc Indian Four in 1935 form, with leaf-spring front forks, unsprung rear wheel, elegant swept 'fenders' (mudguards) and handsome saddle tank. The 74 cu.in engine had four in-line aircooled cylinders and a five-bearing chrome-nickel crankshaft, and this motorcycle, descended from the Henderson-designed Ace 4, cost more than many contemporary U.S. cars.
Left: British baby. The little 'Wolf Cub' of 1936 had a 98cc Villiers two-stroke engine, Albion two-speed gearbox, and pressed steel forks. It cost only £18, complete with electric lighting.
Right: Foreshadowing a future trend that endured for a quarter century, Triumph's first vertical twin cylinder engine was a 649cc ohv unit designed by Val Page and introduced in 1933. Gears instead of chains were used for the primary drive to the four-speed gearbox, and for the timing drive.

Motor Cycle

Left: Two-wheeled car. The curious Whitwood 'Monocar', built by the OEC company of Portsmouth in 1934–35, and offered with engines ranging from 150 to 1000cc. It had wheel steering, OEC low-pivot steering, and two seats in tandem. Right: Big single. A popular bike for fast solo or sidecar work was the elegant P & M Panther, famous as the 'Sloper', with inclined single-cylinder long-stroke two-port ohv engine in 498 or 598cc forms.

Piaggio

Above: An advanced Italian single of 1938, the Gilera model VT SS had an overhead camshaft 500cc engine with light alloy barrel, and rear wheel springing by enclosed coils and friction dampers.

When the Portsmouth-based OEC concern, best known for their low-pivot Duplex steering, fell for the old 'car on two wheels' bait, they did it discreetly under the name Whitwood. The resultant 'Monocar', with a choice of engines from 150 to 1000cc, drew big crowds to their stand at Olympia but few, if any, customers. It had OEC steering, a steering wheel instead of handlebars, two seats in tandem with the engine underneath, plywood bodywork with a Triplex windscreen, and retractable side support wheels. Subsequent design changes included transfer of the engine to the rear, alongside the wheel, but it was all in vain, and the Whitwood 'Monocar' died the usual 'offbeat's death two years later.

## 'Singles' versus 'multis'

By 1936 the motorcycle industry was well out of the doldrums. Despite negative government encouragement in that carefree time when the pound sterling was a power in the world, British exports rose to 19 000 machines, although German motorcyles under the Hitlerian spur were taking an ever-increasing share. The equivalent of a £10 subsidy on each machine exported from the *Reich* was a big incentive, and BMWs, DKWs, NSUs etc were pouring from the factories. The new challenge also made itself felt in international motorcycle racing, so long dominated by the British Norton, Velocette and other singles. It now became a tense battleground between them

Cyril Posthumus

Cyril Posthumus

The unique four-cylinder Nimbus from Denmark, first introduced in 1920, reappeared in 1934 with a new overhead camshaft 750cc aircooled in-line engine having exposed valve rockers and springs. The engine (left) followed MG car fashion in employing the vertical camshaft drive as an armature for the dynamo.

and new German and Italian multis, stimulating design all round. Ever mounting speeds emphasized the crying need for rear-wheel springing, and all participants had adopted it by 1936, while BMW also used telescopic, hydraulically damped front forks, destined to be widely copied.

Since the motorcycle offered such economical and rapid mobility, its manufacture spread to unexpected places. Poland got into the act during the 1930s, contributing the SM shaft-driven ohv '350', the Villiers-engined SHL, sturdy side-valve '600's from PZI and Sokol, and a big 1200cc PZI vee-twin. There was also a 350cc shaft-driven two-stroke called the Lot, and a Moy lightweight with pressed steel backbone. Hungary also had its motorcycle factories, the sporting Meray fitting various bought-out engines. Another make was the Matra, not to be confused with the famous French racing car of recent years, but the best known Hungarian motorbike was the Csepel. It was founded in 1937 by a large engineering firm called Weiss-Manfred in the Csepel district of Budapest, was nationalized after the Second World War, and still builds lively two-strokes today.

From Holland came the Eysink, born with the first motorcycles back in 1898, and using British Villiers and Python engines in the 1930s, and the lightweight Batavus, Sparta, Gazelle and Fama machines employing Ilo, Sachs or Villiers engines. In the Far East the Japanese motorcycle industry was quietly growing, with makers such as Tohatsu and Meguro catering for domestic needs before the War. Denmark imported many British and German motorcycles, but in 1934 that rare in-line aircooled four-cylinder machine, the Copenhagen-built Nimbus, reappeared in modernized form with an unusual flat spring steel frame and an overhead camshaft engine.

## The Danish Nimbus

The makers, Fisker & Nielsen, followed the MG Midget car example by making the vertical camshaft drive-shaft serve double duty in embodying a vertical dynamo. Final drive from the three-speed gearbox was by shaft as on the original Nimbus of 1920, the handlebars were of pressed steel, and the lights were operated by a left-hand twist grip. These ohc 'fours' were used by the

Danish police, post office and army, where they served for dispatch riding and, with sidecar attached, as machine gun carriers, supply vehicles and field ambulances. Although rarely seen beyond Scandinavia and Germany, 12 715 were produced between 1934 and 1959, when manufacture ceased because of the heavy Danish purchase tax, and the makers concentrated on vacuum cleaners and floor polishers.

If the Nimbus was rare, an American motorcycle called the Crocker was infinitely rarer. It was a custom-built 'special' made to order only by A. G. ('Al') Crocker, a Los Angeles machine tool maker, between 1936 and 1941, total output being under 250. Either a 1000 or 1200cc 45° ohv vee-twin engine, with roller bearings throughout, was employed, and cost remained emphatically secondary to quality throughout the machine. With sporting handlebars, light mudguards, neat forks and a shapely 3¾-gallon saddle tank, the Crocker departed notably from the customary American 'heavy look', while its performance was far superior, with a maximum of over 100mph (160km/h) and acceleration to match.

High-performance vee-twins were rare in any country by 1936, but at Olympia that year an all-new British example was a Show sensation. This was the super-sports 998cc Vincent-HRD 'Rapide', designed by the Australian Phil Irving. Its beefy twin-cylinder engine comprised two of the marque's high-camshaft singles set in a 47° vee on a massive crankcase and squeezed, together with twin carburettors, magneto and four-speed gearbox, into the minimum of frame. The power unit had light alloy cylinders with steel liners, and hairpin valve springs. Pivoted triangle-type rear springing was fitted, and there were large-diameter twin drum brakes front and rear to check the pace of this 110mph fire-eater, which weighed only 22 lb (10kg) more than the 500cc single from which it was descended. From the 'Rapide' itself sprang those even more inspiring post-war Vincent twins, the 'Black Shadow' and 'Black Lightning', which might be termed the 'Jaguars' of the two-wheeled world.

Pursuing the analogy the Ariel 'Square Four', shown in 1936 both in 600cc and 1000cc forms, was surely the Rolls-Bentley of the bike world for its dynamo-smooth, effortless performance. Other machines offered performance with less refinement; in probable reaction to the retreating slump there was an outbreak of colourful 'rorty' sports ohv singles with the fashionable upswept exhaust pipes, among them the Matchless 'Clubman', BSA 'Empire Star', Ariel 'Red Hunter' and Triumph 'Tiger'. Even Francis-Barnett, ardent two-stroke exponents, sported a 250cc ohv four-stroke, the 'Stag', while a newcomer, the ohv Stevens, was produced by the former makers of the AJS.

**Above: Grand Luxe machine of the late 1930s was the Ariel 'Square Four', which was enlarged to 600 and 1000cc forms, providing admirably smooth, powerful transport as a solo or combination.**

The new trend for dealers to market their own special models at competitive prices increased, with Pride & Clarke augmenting their 250 and 350cc Red Panthers with the Red Calthorpe, which was the famous 500cc 'Ivory' in cheaper form, the 500cc AJW 'Red Fox', and several Douglas models, while Rennos offered shapely Montgomery-JAPs at inviting prices. '£5 down secures' was an extra lure in advertisements to many an excellent bargain.

### The first 'Speed Twin'

The huge new exhibition hall at Earls Court in London, which, it was claimed, had the largest cantilever roof in Europe, became the

Motor cycle

**Above: Show sensation at Olympia in 1936 was the beefy and decidedly quick Vincent-HRD 'Rapide', with 998cc ohv vee-twin engine having light alloy barrels, hairpin valve springs, rear wheel springing, dual drum brakes, and a maximum of around 110 mph (175 km/h).**
**Below: Lively 'Thumper'. The 350 and 500cc Matchless 'Clubman' models of 1938–39 had high compression ohv single-cylinder engines, the fashionable sporting upswept exhaust pipes, and polished light alloy mudguards. This machine was the basis of the renowned G3 WD Matchless used in the Second World War.**
**Bottom: Built as a prototype but never produced, the 500cc vee-4 AJS with chain-driven overhead camshafts, twin magnetos and hairpin valve springs, was a notably neat and compact ultra-sporting British 'multi' which drew the crowds at the 1935 Motorcycle Show.**

Motor Cycle

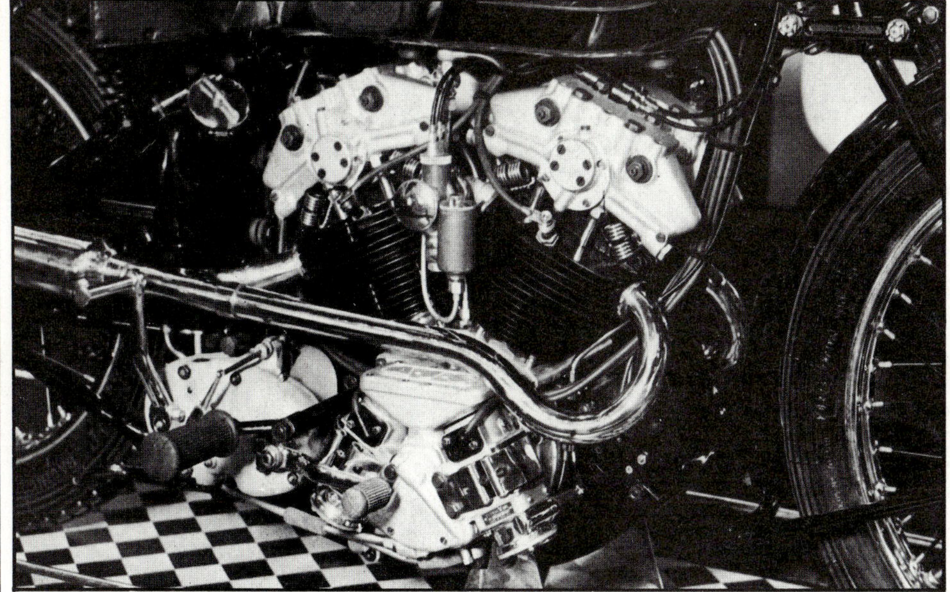

RTHPL

home of the Motorcycle Show from 1937 onward; it afforded more space for individual exhibits than the crowded Olympia halls where so much history had been made. 'Machine of the Show', and of the year, was undoubtedly the Triumph 'Speed Twin', a 498cc vertical twin of such clean, compact design that it resembled a two-port single in profile, and fitted into the standard 'Tiger 90' frame. Moreover it weighed 5 lb (2.25kg) less than the single and cost only £5 more! Motorcyclists being a cautious, conservative lot, the new Triumph didn't instantly sweep the single-cylinder motorbike off the market, but it certainly gave tradition a jolt and set a design format that was to endure for 30 years.

Its designer was Edward Turner, creator of the Ariel 'Square Four', and like Val Page on Triumph's earlier 640cc twin, Turner employed a crankshaft with side by side crankpins, the pistons rising and falling together. The crankshaft was built-up with a central flywheel, and the overhead valves were actuated through twin gear-driven camshafts, pushrods and rockers. The layout had much in its favour; the side-by-side cylinders took no more space lengthwise than a single, yet both got a full measure of cooling air. It offered much of the smoothness and urge of a 'four' with less weight, complication and cost, and but for a justified preoccupation with the approaching war among major manufacturers, Turner's vertical twin would surely have been copied much earlier than it was.

So neat and unobtrusive was its appearance that the more naive visitors to Earls Court passed by and made instead for the Brough Superior, where George Brough again obliged with a 'Show surprise'. This time it was a transverse vee-twin driving through an Austin Seven car-type synchromesh gearbox and final chain. The engine was a 990cc side valve AMC (Associated Motor Cycles, the Woolwich-based group comprising Matchless, AJS and, from 1937, Sunbeam) as used on Morgan three-wheelers, but the crankcase and gearbox were enclosed *à la* New Hudson by shielding, which at the front embodied a handsome domed oil tank. Another commendable feature was the excellent plunger rear springing, but only one example of this Brough was ever made.

Right: Rare foreigners. The Husqvarna was a well-built Swedish machine which earned international fame in prewar road racing. This Model 112 TV sports of 1936 has a single-cylinder ohv 496cc Husqvarna engine, four-speed gearbox with foot-change, and Bosch magneto.
Below: "This we must have" say two German potential customers on viewing the 1938 flat-twin shaft-drive Zündapp in the showroom window.
Opposite, top: Velocette publicity for 1937 featured the popular ohc 350cc KTS model. Veloce Ltd were pioneers in marketing road models with overhead camshaft engines and foot gearchange, developed through racing.

ZÜNDAPP

„Die müssen wir haben!.."

ZÜNDAPP-MOTORRÄDER
VON RM. 540.– BIS RM. 1495.–

ZÜNDAPP
WERKE G·M·B·H NÜRNBERG

Cyril Posthumus

Below: Power of the hour. Having firmly established the vertical twin engine as a smooth, powerful and compact unit, Triumph augmented their standard 'Speed Twin' with the higher-performance 'Tiger 100' sports model in 1938.

Motor Cycle

## The threat of war

As the 'guns before butter' policies of Fascist Germany and Italy intensified, so the rest of Europe had to 'think military' as well, and the British motorcycle industry inevitably became involved. Dispatch riders' machines were ordered in quantity from Norton, Matchless, Royal Enfield and others for the various services, while many firms took on other forms of war work such as engineering. This unavoidable diversification encroached on civilian motorcycle production, and the 1938 Earls Court Show, coming as it did shortly after the Munich crisis, had a decidedly preoccupied air about it.

Yet there were some important exhibits. Ariel introduced a plunger-type rear springing system with swinging links that kept wheel spindle travel in an arc, thereby ensuring constant chain tension. This springing became an optional extra on all models over 250cc, and made the newest 600 and 1000cc 'Square Fours' even more desirable. Then Triumph produced a higher performance edition of their 'Speed Twin', having a higher compression engine, silver instead of 'plum' finish, and the name 'Tiger 100'. Two old companies, Calthorpe and New Imperial, ran into financial straits, the former going into liquidation while the latter passed under the wing of Jack Sangster, proprietor of Ariel and Triumph. Alas, they were later sold off again, never to build another motorcycle.

It fell, as ever, to the irrepressible George Brough to provide the one real Show surprise—his last, as things regrettably transpired, and probably his best. The Brough Superior 'Golden Dream', jointly designed by Brough himself, H. J. Hatch of the Blackburne engine concern, and racing motorcyclist/driver/engineer F. W. Dixon, had a 996cc flat-four aircooled engine. In action it amounted to two transverse flat twin units, one above the other, with coupled crankshafts giving remarkable smoothness, silence and flexibility. Totally enclosed ohv were operated by chain-driven camshafts and short pushrods, and twin Amal carburettors were employed.

Final drive was by enclosed shaft and

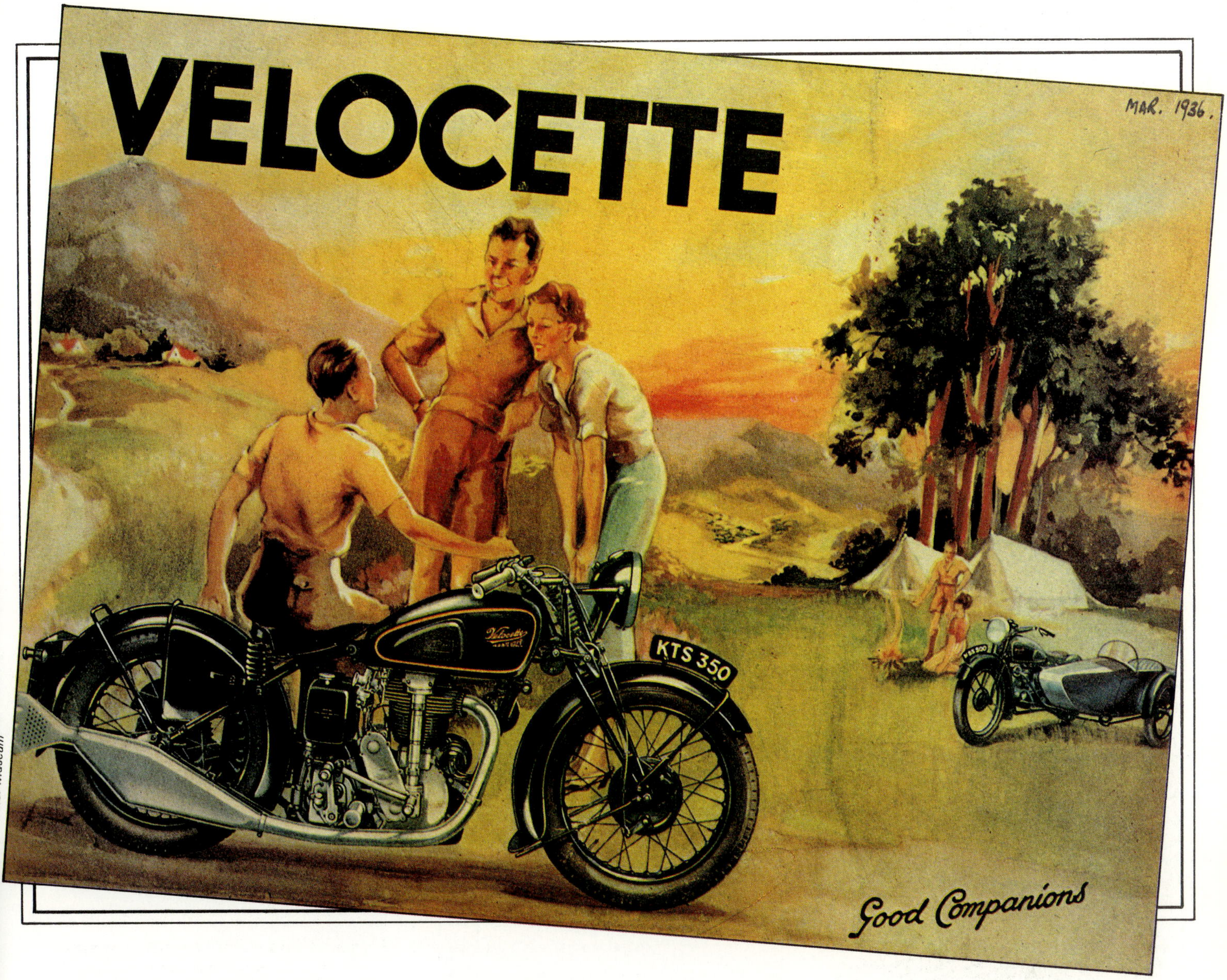

worm gearing, in conjunction with Brough-type plunger rear springing. With deeply valanced mudguards, Castle-type front forks, and a broad saddle, the 'Dream' had a certain transatlantic heavinesss about it, offset by its low build and symmetry of components. It was an expensive motorcycle both to build and to buy, at £185, yet it was the most original of all the Brough Superior 'specials'. Unfortunately the times were against this potentially brilliant British design, and less than half a dozen had been built when war terminated further development.

With hostilities looming ever closer, the international road racing scene indicated ever more clearly that the traditional single-cylinder motorcycle had met its match in the quest for speed regardless of cost. The once invincible ohc Nortons, 'top dogs' since 1931, failed to win a single major event, the supercharged German BMW twins or the Italian four-cylinder Gileras taking every 500cc race, including the Isle of Man Senior TT and the Ulster GP on Norton's 'home ground'. Other Continental multis such as the DKW and NSU further menaced the dating British defence, pointing up the hard fact that multi-cylinder engines were the format for the future, while the once dominant single would gradually be relegated to the smallest capacity classes.

But all this lay in the next quarter-century, and in the acute tension of 1939 future motorcycle design trends were academic to the more immediate international crises, which finally exploded into open conflict in September. Once again men and machines found themselves plunged into battle, and the peacetime chrome and cellulose disappeared beneath the universal khaki war-paint.

**Below: A flat-four of great promise was the Brough Superior 'Dream', with 996cc aircooled engine with two coupled crankshafts, plunger-type rear springing, and shaft final drive. The outbreak of war ended development after only six had been built.**

*Vintage Motor Cycle Club*

# STORMY TIMES

"We have got something to shout about today . . . here is an industry in which Britain is 'cock of the walk' . . ."

James Callaghan, MP, Parliamentary Secretary to the Minister of Transport, when opening the Earls Court Motorcycle Show, 1949

The advent of war in September 1939 suspended all progress in motorcycle design for the six years' duration of hostilities. As in the First World War, motorcycles served a vital military role, not only on dispatch riding duties as solos but as reconnaissance and supply vehicles and mobile machine gun or mortar carriers in sidecar form. Hundreds of thousands of special machines were used by combatants in all theatres of war, from sub-zero ice and snow conditions to desert and jungle heat.

Little of this could be foreseen at the beginning, when apart from black-out rules requiring the fitting of headlamp masks, petrol (gasoline) rationing, and the introduction of 'Pool' petrol (a dismal all-vehicle fuel of about 72 octane), the switch to a war footing in Allied countries was little more 'immediate' than it had been in 1914. Production of civilian motorcycles continued on a reduced scale, several manufacturers hopefully fielding 1940 models until the 'phoney war' period ended abruptly the following spring. There was an inevitable reversion to austerity lightweights, encouraged by the availability of Villiers' newest 'flat top' piston two-stroke engines, including a new 98cc unit for autocycles, and had there been a 1939 Earls Court Show, it would have been a lean and rather dreary affair.

### Into khaki

Major British manufacturers such as Norton, BSA, Matchless, Ariel, Triumph and Royal Enfield were fully occupied with War Office orders, though most still nominally listed civilian models. In fact Triumph's vertical twins were attracting particular attention in the United States, where peace still reigned, and Royal Enfield contrived to introduce a sports ohv 500 with aluminium cylinder and Vacrit liner. Sunbeam, now associated with the Matchless and AJS companies, listed a full range from 250 to 600cc, all having their new high-camshaft engine in which a single chain drove both the camshaft and the magdyno, while OEC offered some clean ohv models using AMC(Matchless) engines.

There were several new spring frames, mostly of the plunger type, although New Imperial's well-known pivot system reappeared on a range of 250, 350 and 500cc ohv singles listed 'on paper' by the new proprietor, Jack Sangster, who had transferred the factory from Birmingham to Coventry. Alas, this marked the end for a famous British make, since Sangster sold off the business shortly after to a concern having no interest in motorcycle production. James, Excelsior and Francis-Barnett were among users of the new flat-top Villiers engines, and had anything at the hypothetical 1939 Show rated a 'surprise' it would have been that Panther had supplemented their famous 'Slopers' with 1940 Redwing 90(500cc) and 100(600cc) models having vertical motors. The impact of this apparent heresy was largely lost as the European war worsened. New spring frames featuring quadrupled $\frac{1}{4}$-elliptic leaf springs, designed by Granville Bradshaw, were an optional Redwing extra, but these, too, went largely unnoticed and never, in fact, saw a production line.

On the War Department side, the value of competitions, and in particular trials and cross-country racing (then known as scrambling but nowadays called motocross) became evident. Apart from their dull khaki finish, the service versions of the 350cc ohv Matchless and Ariel closely resembled pre-war competition jobs, with high ground clearance,

*Imperial War Museum*

Imperial War Museum

Service machines of all nations. **Left:** French forces used the BMW-style transverse flat-twin Gnome-Rhône during their brief war. **Opposite:** A popular British WD bike was the 350cc 'high cam' Velocette MAF. The riders here are two famous racing motorcyclists, J.H. White and F.L. Frith, both of whom were highly qualified Army instructors in dispatch riding. **Below:** Eighth Army men in the Middle East trying out a captured German BMW combination. **Bottom:** A Russian dispatch rider delivers a message; his mount is a copy of the German 100cc two-stroke DKW.

upright riding positions and spirited performance despite military 'compromise' gear ratios. Royal Enfield also contributed a lively ohv dispatch rider's bike as well as a 350cc side-valve, while bigger side-valve 'plonkers came from BSA (the M20) and Norton (the 16H). The latter firm also developed a special 633cc combination based on their famous 'Big Four' side-valve 'single' with sidecar wheel drive, while a rarer militarized high-camshaft Velocette, the MAF, was much coveted by discerning dispatch riders.

### Foreign service bikes

At the outbreak of war, Germany had many 100cc two-stroke DKW lightweights for road messenger work; the same marque also

Imperial War Museum

Imperial War Museum

produced a sturdy 350, while larger transverse-twin BMWs and Zündapps, and a mixture of NSUs, Victorias and TWNs all did arduous duty on behalf of the *Wehrmacht*. During their brief war, the French equipment included Gnome-Rhône transverse flat-twins and René-Gillet vee-twins, but the bulk of these, and other Continental equipment such as Belgian Saroléa, FN and Gillet, and Danish Nimbus machines, fell into German hands as the *blitzkrieg* raged across the West.

Italy's military motorcycles were a heterogeneous collection including ohc Bianchis, side-valve spring-frame Gileras and Bianchis, the Guzzi 'Alce' 500cc horizontal single with side inlet and overhead exhaust valves, and sundry commandeered civilian machines. Many of the 'Alce' solos carried two seats, the rear passenger having a compact pair of handlebars to hold on to; an ungainly three-wheeled version, the 'Trialce' had a broad folding platform body, and an even beefier variant served as a mobile gun carrier.

The Russians scarcely had a motorcycle industry when war began, but the Moskva national works, founded in 1940, very

Right: Belgian army equipment included many of these impressive 1000cc transverse flat-twin Type M12 FN combinations with sidecar wheel drive. After the collapse of Belgium in 1940 many were used by the Germans. Below: America's seemingly indestructible Harley-Davidson side-valve big twins served with the Allied Forces in all war zones. Note the rifle bracket, front tool box and rear panniers on this 45 cu. in MP version.

Cyril Posthumus

Imperial War Museum

logically and swiftly copied captured examples of the side-valve transverse twin 750cc BMW, complete with shaft drive, spring frame and telescopic front forks. This figured chiefly as a combination, but some solos also served, while under the Lease-Lend scheme the U.S.S.R was also supplied with Velocette MAF, Matchless G3 and BSA M20 machines from Britain. Before they themselves entered the war, the United States supplied numerous 45 cu. in. (750cc) Harley-Davidson and Indian vee-twins to Allied forces, and sent thousands more over when their own troops joined the fray. Both were massive vehicles of forbidding aspect; fitted out with foot-boards, big pannier bags, crash bars and other equipment such as sub-machine gun mounts, they were extremely heavy and ungainly, though virtually indestructible.

### Teledraulics

Early military Matchless G3s were fitted with girder-type front forks, but from 1941 these were replaced by new 'Teledraulic' single-tube telescopic type with hydraulic damping, as used by BMW since 1935. Advantages other than aesthetic included reduced unsprung weight, enclosure of parts, and better fork action than the triangulated girder type. Although Matchless did not invent the principle, which indeed was pioneered by Alfred Scott many years before BMW took it up, they were instrumental in popularizing its use, and the 'Teledraulic' fork rates as one of the few design benefits to emerge from the 1939–45 holocaust. On the 'contra' account, a casualty of Coventry's bombing was a promising Triumph 350cc side-valve vertical twin, the 3T/W, production of which had to be deferred.

While the rigours of war generally seemed to demand strong and clumsy machinery, an unusual Allied requirement was the development of special lightweight motorcycles for their airborne divisions. These were built in Britain by Royal Enfield and James around

**Right: The ingenious little 98cc Excelsior 'Welbike' was designed specifically to provide quick mobility for paratroops. They were parachuted from aircraft in special containers; folding handlebars and seat pillar made the 'Welbike' more compact.**
**Below: One of Rommel's scout teams in the Western Desert in Libya with their 750cc BMW combination; note the telescopic forks.**

*Imperial War Museum*

the faithful 125cc Villiers two-stroke engine, for transporting in Horsa and other gliders together with troops. They were also dropped by parachute in special tubular crates, and proved invaluable in providing quick mobility for key troops in battle areas. The specification called for a dry weight of about 140 lb (63kg) as well as folding footrests and handlebars to facilitate stowing. James's model was nicknamed the 'Clockwork Mouse' and Royal Enfield's the 'Flying Flea'.

The Americans commissioned a similar lightweight from the Simplex Manufacturing Co. of New Orleans. Called the Servi-Cycle, this, too, had a 125cc two-stroke engine, based on a late pre-war civilian design old-fashioned in having belt drive, with a pedal-operated 'clutch' which simply slipped the belt. 'Jump' starting was employed instead of a kickstarter, but such crudities could pass on machines which were largely expendable.

Another special product the Allies employed was an even smaller portable 'run-about' or 'parascooter' to be dropped from aircraft. Excelsior of Birmingham called theirs the 'Welbike'; it had a 98cc two-stroke power unit, single speed transmission, a tiny cradle frame, very small wheels, and folding handlebars and seat pillar. The American equivalent was the Cushman, built by a Nebraska offshoot of the Evinrude engine firm. Its four-stroke engine was adapted from an outboard unit, and drove through two speeds and chain final drive. Apart from such special-purpose bikes, both the Allies and the Axis made a partial switch from motorcycle units to cross-country cars as the war continued. The American four-wheel drive Willys Jeep replaced the crude Harley-Davidsons and Indians, while Germany's complex two-wheel drive eight-speed hydraulic-braked

Motor cycle

Left and below: With the return of peace Matchless of Woolwich were quickly into production with this smart black-and-chrome civilian edition of their famous WD G3/L with 'Teledraulic' forks.

BMW and Zündapp combinations gave way to the Volkswagen 'Kubel' four-wheel drive aircooled flat-four.

### The reckoning

By the end of it all some 450 000 motorcycles had been built by British firms alone, a number equalled, if not excelled, by Germany. With countless other war commodities manufactured on a similar giant scale, it was small wonder that, when peace came at last, most of the combatants were not only physically but also financially exhausted. After the first fine careless raptures of VE and VJ days came the harsh reckoning, and the anticlimax of urgent economy and export drives if nations were to extricate themselves from acute financial stringencies. Only the United States emerged with economic stability, and it was on their currency, the 'almighty dollar', that many nations were to depend for recovery.

Although the slump and mass unemployment that had followed the First World War were averted this time, political turmoil and a world shortage of materials and fuel, including petrol, added to the monetary problems and greatly hampered recovery after 1945. In Britain the 'export or die' edict affected everything. Despite dire shortages at home, goods of all kinds, with cars and motorcycles high on the list, were rushed abroad as fast as they could be produced in exchange for vital dollars or other stable currencies.

A miserly petrol ration of two or three gallons per month, for under or over 250cc motorcycles, granted in 1945, was eloquent of those austerity days, and the cheap, frugal lightweight was much sought as a tool of travel. Unwittingly taunting bike-starved Britons, Triumphs were first to announce a post-war programme around their two fine twins, very much for 'export only', plus a new 350cc version, the 3T, all with new telescopic forks. Matchless, still geared for production of their Teledraulic-forked War Department model, lost no time in producing smart, black-finished 350 and 500cc civilian successors.

Both James and Royal Enfield offered 125cc two-strokes clearly derived from their wartime glider-borne lightweights, while an enterprising newcomer to the industry, Brockhouse Engineering of Southport, announced the Corgi runabout, a 'civvy' version of the Excelsior 'Welbike' parascooter. Its 98cc Excelsior 'Spryt' two-stroke engine propelled it at 30 mph (48km/h) on one gear only (two were later fitted), but the price was a basic £52, which was some £8 to £10 more than most contemporary British 98cc autocycles such as the Cyc-Auto, Excelsior 'Autobyk', Francis-Barnett 'Power-bike', New Hudson 'Autocycle', Raynal 'Auto' and Norman 'Motobyk'. All these were unexciting utility machines forming an essential part of the 1946 motorcycle picture.

More cheering was the return of Ariel with 'Red Hunter' sports ohvs, a 600cc sidevalve and their splendid 1000cc 'Square

RTHPL

Four', all little changed since 1939. Norton and BSA also returned, first with brightened up editions of their war models, and then with livelier ohv models, the Nortons sporting new 'Roadholder' telescopic forks evolved through racing before the war. Other makes hinted at enticing things to come in their advertisements, while struggling hard with bureaucracy to secure steel allocations and other essentials before resuming production. This was harder for small firms, which were required to show full order books to convince the authorities, and had to 'join the queue' for vital parts in short supply.

### America buys British

Naturally the 'plum' models were exported to the United States, where they made considerable impression on motorcyclists more accustomed to heaving their clumsy domestic big twins around. The lighter, faster, more accelerative and decidedly more comely British vertical twins had great appeal, and demand quickly outran supply, with long waiting lists building up at dealers. All this meant vital dollars for the United Kingdom, while the patient British motorcyclist waited on and on for *his* post-war machine. "Please

**Below: Top choice for many ex-servicemen buying a new motorcycle was the 500cc Triumph 'Speed Twin' in its postwar trim with telescopic front forks and a maroon finish. The British police used Triumph twins for over thirty years.**

**Bottom: Invisible suspension. The ingenious Triumph 'spring hub' introduced in 1948 after earlier success in road racing. The wheel spindle ran in guides governed by coil springs, but travel and alignment limitations caused replacement by swinging arm suspension in 1954.**

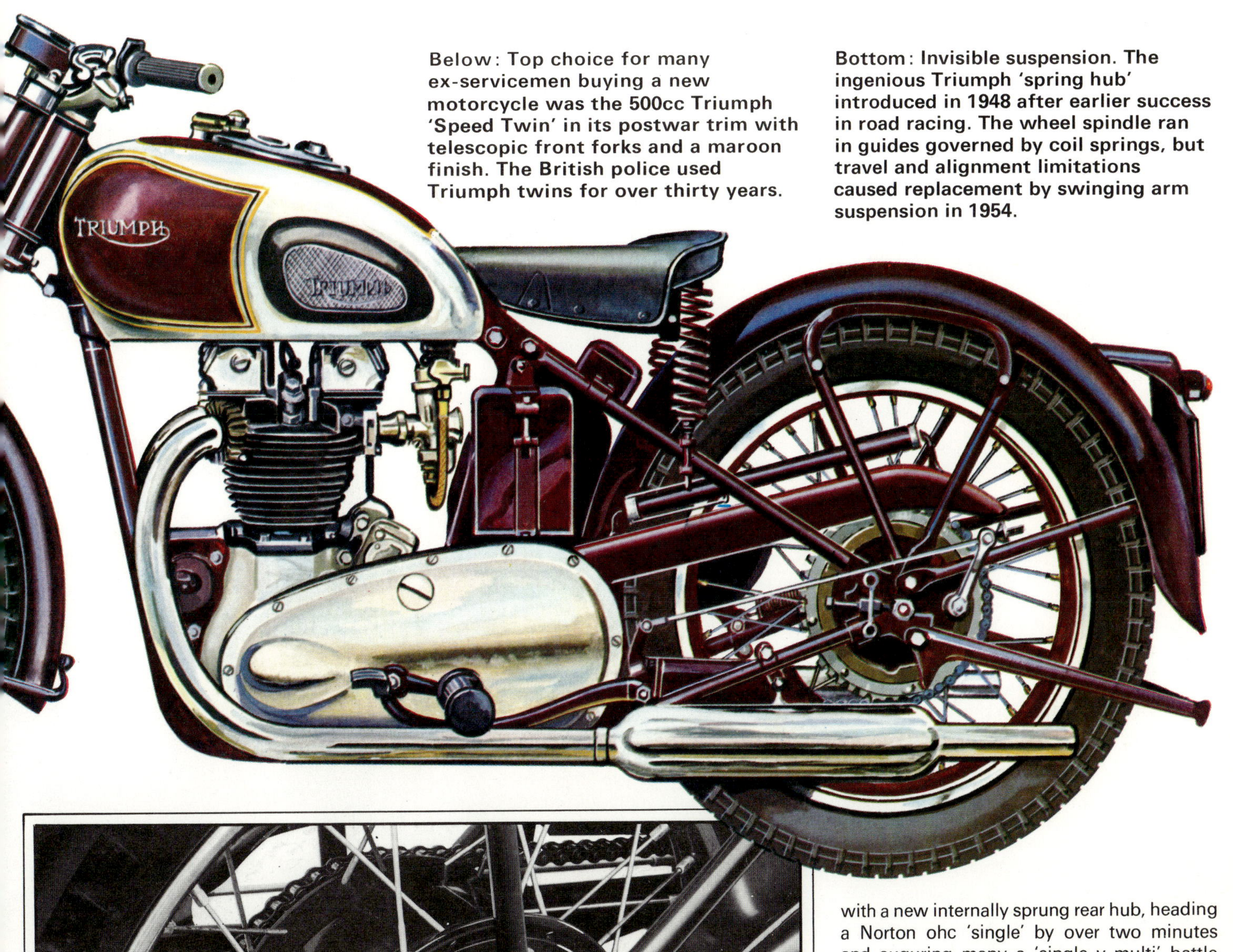


*Motor Cycle*

. . . " began a Norton advertisement, "extend your forebearance. Be Patient – and be assured that everyone in the Norton organisation is as anxious as you are to get you *your* machine."

Meantime there was some comfort from the next best thing, a reconditioned and resprayed ex-WD machine such as the 350cc side-valve Royal Enfield at £55 basic plus £14 13s 4d extra for a new bureaucratic invention called purchase tax. But gradually things improved. The urgent need to make and export forcibly cleared the way; material supply blockages were eased, and the many 'made out' components that form a motorcycle—castings, pressings, forgings, springs, electrics, tires, saddles, lighting, etc, began to flow, although manufacturers often had to compromise their wants with availability in the way of chains, gearboxes, etc.

Motorcycling being so closely linked with sport, the return of racing was a vital symptom of rising morale. It began with amateur meetings, several of them on redundant wartime airfields, and by 1946 the Manx GP was revived on the Isle of Man TT course. The winning Senior (500cc) machine was a racing edition of the Triumph vertical twin with a new internally sprung rear hub, heading a Norton ohc 'single' by over two minutes and auguring many a 'single-v-multi' battle to come, to the ultimate benefit of design.

That same year brought three important new British road models, all of them twins, from Vincent-HRD, Douglas and Sunbeam. The big-twin high-camshaft Vincent-HRD 'Rapide' which had enlivened the 1936 Earls Court Show reappeared in much improved Series B form, its most striking change being employment of the engine as a stressed part of the frame, P & M Panther style, by bolting special head lugs to the frame, with long studs passing through the cylinder to the crankcase. Meticulous weight-saving on this very powerful yet tractable motorcycle gave it searing acceleration and a 112mph (180 km/h) maximum, making it easily the world's fastest standard production motorcycle. Roadholding, steering, braking and finish were to top standards, and the waiting list for this eminently desirable property grew long indeed despite a British price of over £290.

Douglas of Bristol, famous for their First World War WD machines, received no War Office orders for motorcycles in the Second World War; their flat-twin design was deemed too dated. Instead they produced aircraft parts, generating sets, stationary engines and industrial trucks, but returned to motorcycles in 1946 with a new design. It was not wholly new, for the 350cc pushrod ohv engine took the traditional Douglas flat-twin configuration, although mounted transversely like a BMW—or, Douglas's own abortive Endeavour

Cyril Posthumus

of 1935 or, of course, the 1920 ABC. Power passed through a car-type clutch, four-speed gearbox and chain final drive, and the major novelty lay in the frame springing.

At the rear this was by a swinging arm linked with torsion bars enclosed in the lower frame tubes, while at the front the torsion bars were enclosed in the tubular fork legs and connected by bell cranks to leading links. During development some shortcomings were encountered in this system, chiefly in restricted travel; accordingly the torsion bars were replaced by coil springs with hydraulic damping, the lower coils being tapered by precision grinding to give progressive action. Low unsprung weight was one advantage of the resultant 'Radiadraulic' fork as it was called.

### An advanced Sunbeam

Sunbeam's new model, the S7, epitomized the wartime 'dream bike' of many Britons. It had an elegant 490cc in-line aircooled vertical twin engine with chain-driven oh camshaft operating parallel ohv, a four-speed gearbox in unit, and shaft final drive. Plunger-type rear springing and telescopic front forks completed a thoroughly up-to-date specification, and the S7 had notably wide wheels carrying huge 4.75in (12cm) section tires which, in conjunction with deeply valanced mudguards, gave it a heavy look. It was essentially a 'grand tourer', the rubber-mounted engine proving exceptionally smooth, silent and flexible; the wheels were quickly detachable and interchangeable, and early models were finished in the traditional Sunbeam black and gold. A more sporting variant, the S8, had smaller tires, lighter mudguards, lighter forks and higher compression.

Sunbeam's post-war proprietors, the BSA group, had long intended launching a vertical twin themselves. War Office contracts prevented its release before the war, and it only reached the production stage by late 1946. Unlike the Sunbeam the engine followed Triumph style in being mounted transversely; a clean and simple 499cc unit, it had pushrod ohv actuated by a single camshaft. It was followed early in 1947 by another broadly similar vertical twin, the 498cc Ariel, which was distinguished by a one-piece forged crankshaft and light alloy connecting rods. Still other vertical twins came within the next two and a half years from Norton, AJS, Matchless and Royal Enfield in Britain, and yet others overseas. Commendable points of the layout including smoother power delivery, compactness, amenable carburation and relatively moderate production costs, with the cylinders in a monobloc casting and simple valve gear.

A measure of the British industry's recovery was apparent in the export figures. Despite a lengthy shut-down due to the serious fuel crisis, 55 072 motorcycles were exported between September 30, 1946 and the same date in 1947. Most of them went to the United States, others to the Commonwealth, Belgium, Holland, Sweden, Switzerland, China and South American countries. With factories working all out to meet demand on a sellers' market, the annual 'shop window' of the Motorcycle Show would have been irrelevant and wasteful of time and money, and accordingly the hard-pressed industry decided against holding one in 1947.

On the ravaged European Continent the struggle for recovery was more dramatic. The French industry had been pillaged during the Nazi occupation and further decimated during the Allied invasion. Their surviving resources could produce little but a mass of 'flea-powered' *vélomoteurs* and motorized bicycles, yet such was Gallic resilience that they contrived to hold a Paris Motorcycle Show in conjunction with the car *Salon* in 1946, displaying several ambitious if sometimes improbable prototypes of advanced concept.

The Italians also managed a *Salone Motociclismo* at Turin late that year, when it was noticeable that some names formerly exalted in Italy's air force, such as Breda, Caproni and Macchi now appeared on the tanks of humble motorcycles. Other new names included Morini, Moretti, MV-Agusta and Parilla, most of them offering the exquisite little ohv or ohc four-stroke engines which Italian engineers have always excelled at. Yet none was of greater portent than another new make, Vespa, destined to precipitate a new 'scooter age' and make a name for itself.

### The scooter phenomenon

Whereas the scooters of the earlier 'age' between 1919 and 1922 died off through poor performance and unreliability, the new Italian machines had lively, durable little engines, proper multi-speed gearboxes and modern production technology to back them. Moreover, in a country where public transport was notoriously poor, teenagers, women and others who were interested solely in handy, dependable independent transport without wanting to know how it functioned, flocked to buy scooters. They had open frames with flat footboards, reliable enclosed engines, easy-change wheels and adequate protection for riders to wear town clothes yet keep clean. With combined seating they carried two as easily as one, plus a modicum of luggage, yet they were economic on fuel and oil, relatively cheap to buy, and required no road tax.

National Motor Museum

First of a swiftly multiplying breed was the Vespa (meaning 'wasp') which drew enormous attention at Turin in 1946. It was the product of the famous Piaggio aero-engine concern, who 40 years earlier had built British Napier cars under licence, and whose radial aero-engines had powered

Piaggio

Left: Italian pioneer. The prototype of over 5 million Vespa scooters built so far, revolutionizing personal transport. Far left: Flat-single. Low build was an advantage on the Italian 500cc Guzzi Model GTW of 1949, with its horizontal single-cylinder ohc engine, telescopic front forks and unusual rear springing. Below: One of the most exciting new post-war models was the revised Vincent-HRD 'Rapide'. The twin cylinders of its 998cc vee engine served as frame members while on the later Series C, shown here, light alloy 'Girdraulic' forks replaced the friction-damped Bramptons of pre-war days. Bottom: A postwar British twin with a difference was the Douglas T35, its 350cc flat-twin ohv engine being installed transversely.

Italian flying boats and bombers during the Second World War. The designer, Corrado d'Ascanio, tackled his new brief as an aircraft engineer totally uninhibited by current motorcycle practice. The frame was formed from steel pressings spot-welded together. The engine, enclosed with detachable side panels, was a 98cc (later 125cc) two-stroke single, mounted well off-centre to the right and driving through a tiny three-speed gearbox direct to the rear wheel. Both wheels were mounted on stub axles, which meant that they could be removed from one side without disturbing the drive, making maintenance, puncture repairs, etc a simple matter.

In a year during which much time was spent tooling up, nearly 2500 Vespas were built at Pontedera and snapped up by an eager public. In 1947 they produced over 7000, and other business eyes focused keenly on this lucrative new facet of economy motorcycling. The Innocenti company of Milan, makers of presses, rolling mills and other industrial equipment, laid down a 123cc scooter design in 1947. Its frame was of steel tubing, and its engine was exposed as on the British Corgi, although Innocenti's scooter,

Motor cycle

**Right: Americans accustomed to heavy vee-twin Indian motorcycles were surprised when the new 440cc 'Super Scout' was announced in 1948. Its European-style vertical twin ohv engine, telescopic front forks, plunger-type rear springing and general 'cobby' looks were a revolutionary breakaway for the old-established marque from Springfield, Mass. They could not save it from extinction by 1953.**

Motor Cycle

called the Lambretta after Lambrate, the Milan suburb in which their factory lay, was infinitely more refined. It had a three-speed gearbox with foot-change, shaft final drive, sprung wheels, twin saddles and a neat one-piece pressed headlamp nacelle-cum-handle-bars and instruments.

Clearly there was room for both the Vespa and the Lambretta. Sales boomed, not only in Italy but in France, Germany, Spain and elsewhere on the European Continent. But not in Britain, which had led the earlier boom, and was perhaps over-wary of the scooter this time. True, the Swallow Sidecar Co. of Walsall, founded in the 1920s by William Lyons of subsequent Jaguar car fame, launched a scooter in 1947 called the Gadabout. It had an enclosed 125cc Villiers engine and three speeds, but at £99 inclusive of purchase tax it was expensive compared with contemporary British minibikes, and this combined with the innate British resistance to a new fashion counted against it.

In other European countries, the scooter proliferated; Bernardet and Terrot of France, DKW and NSU (under Lambretta licence) and Puch of Austria were early on the scene, followed in the 1950s—the scooter's 'golden age'—by a veritable flood of makers. From Germany came Zündapp, Durkopp, Maico, Goggo, Kreidler, Adler, TWN, Victoria and the famous aircraft firm of Heinkel; from France came Motobécane, Peugeot, Manurrhin (DKW under licence) and others; Italy added the Motobi, Rumi and more to the flood of Vespas and Lambrettas, and Britain joined in, somewhat late in the day, with machines by Dunkley, Bond, Raleigh, Piatti, Triumph, BSA, Dayton, Velocette, etc.

None of the British scooters was really successful, and Douglas Motors made a better choice when, in 1949, they secured a licence to build the Vespa in Britain, using British equipment such as an Amal carburettor, Lucas electrics and a BTH flywheel magneto. Production was under way by March 1951 and soon 200 machines a week were coming off the line. Experts declare that the scooter fashion is now past its peak, but so far over 5 million Vespas alone have been built by Piaggio in Italy and by licensees in Spain, several African and Malaysian countries, Pakistan, Indonesia and Taiwan.

### The first postwar Show

The British Motorcycle Show was revived at Earls Court in November 1948. The first in ten years, it broke all attendance records with over 130 000 paying visitors, and among the 29 British makers it was good to see Panther back with modernized editions of their famous long-stroke 'Sloper' single, looking suave with new Dowty 'Oleomatic' telescopic forks. The same type forks appeared on a resurrection of the famous 596cc Scott 'Flying Squirrel' watercooled two-stroke twin. Velocette, too, sprang a big surprise with their new LE, an up-to-the-minute utility bike with a 149cc transverse twin side-valve watercooled engine, unit construction and shaft drive passing through one swinging arm of the rear suspension.

Front forks were telescopic, the frame was

Motor Cycle

**Left: 'The Noddy bike'. Velocette's famous LE, with 192cc watercooled transverse twin side-valve engine and shaft drive. Footboards, legshields and a hand starter featured, and this utility machine was extremely quiet and tractable to ride. It was used extensively by the British police. Below: American extravaganza as exemplified by the big, beefy 1950 Harley-Davidson Electra-Glide with 1200cc ohv vee-twin engine, telescopic front forks, and some typical 'cowboy' equipment favoured in the U.S. Opposite, below: One of Britain's first post-war scooters was the Swallow 'Gadabout', introduced in 1947 with 125cc Villiers two-stroke engine and three-speed gearbox. It lacked the attractive lines of its Italian rivals.**

of pressed steel backbone type, and coil ignition, a hand starter and footboards all figured. The LE was not cheap to build nor to buy, but fortunately the police used it extensively in 192cc form, when it gained the nickname 'the Noddy bike'. A cheaper lightweight was the new BSA Bantam with 123cc unit construction two-stroke engine based on the German DKW design. Triumph's unusual rear 'spring hub' was now an optional extra on their twins, although the advantage of total enclosure was offset by limited spring travel, lack of hydraulic damping and a tendency to tilt when cornering hard; five years later it gave way to swinging arms. Vincent-HRD made British mouths water with another 'export priority' fire-eater, a high-performance 'Rapide' called the 'Black Lightning', with a most attractive all-black finish including engine and brakes, and an awe-inspiring 122mph (195km/h) maximum.

With European design increasingly influencing the American scene, the two U.S. makers took defensive measures. Harley-Davidson cleaned up their lumpish 1000 and 1200cc twins, fitted telescopic forks and introduced some bright new colour schemes. Indian went much further, renouncing 40 years of Springfield tradition to produce a European-styled ohv vertical twin, the 'Warrior', in 400 and 440cc sizes (later also 500cc) with coil ignition, plunger rear springing and front 'teles'. It could not match European performance, and did not survive long. Sadly the Indian concern, founded in 1901, came to a standstill in 1951, when control passed to the English Brockhouse Company. They added a monobloc side-valve 250 to the range, but the last genuine Indian-built motorcycle left the Springfield line in 1953.

Britain's fight back to prosperity suffered a severe setback in late 1949 when Labour Premier Clement Attlee had to impose fresh financial curbs to offset a financial crisis. These included the total abolition of the basic petrol ration—four years after the

Allies 'won' the war!—while manufacturers had to rationalize production and save on development and tooling costs. Ironically, while Britain groaned under new, politically-precipitated austerities, nations which had met defeat in the war began a sensational recovery.

Germany, split into Eastern and Western Zones after 1945, found itself down and out, most of its factories destroyed during hostilities or emptied of their machinery as subsequent reparations. Credits were scarce and money even scarcer, but by 1949 there were strong signs of recovery. Apart from some Horex 350cc police machines, all post-war German motorcycles at the time were limited to 250cc top capacity, though to build any at all demanded extremes of expediency. Machine tools were improvised or bought second-hand, materials were scarce, factories had to be rebuilt, and skilled labour found.

As an example, the famous BMW marque of Munich began post-war activities in reduced circumstances. They made pots and pans, baking machinery, air compressors and farm tools before getting back to motorcycles in 1949. As leading radial aero-engine makers during the war they still had quantities of unmachined light alloy cylinders and other parts; they melted these down for the alloy, which they then built into a single-cylinder 248cc shaft-drive model produced at the rate of 50 a week by April 1949. The DKW concern, whose roots were in Saxony, had to split into East and West German factors as IFA (later becoming MZ) and DKW respectively, while a Russian-built 125cc edition emerged under the Moskva trademark.

## Many newcomers

A Polish 'national' motorcycle factory was founded in Warsaw under the initials WFM, producing utilitarian lightweights, and another 'behind the curtain' nation, Czechoslovakia, built the Hurikan, Manet and Eso as well as the better known CZ and Jawa. Wherever there were roads, indeed, motorcycles were required, and countries emerging after the war with new-won technical 'know how' took up manufacture to combat imports. Spain entered the industry with Latin fervour and soon gained international fame, the Montesa marque, renowned in modern competitions, being founded in 1945, followed by Lube, Febo, Motobic, Ossa, Derbi and others. Austria contributed the now well known KTM, while Hungary revived the Csepel and Sweden the Husqvarna. Even Norway produced a machine, the 125cc Tempo two-stroke, while the new state of Israel launched the ZWI from Tel Aviv in 1952.

But the most significant flowering of all was in Japan, stricken by the atomic bomb in 1945. Even in that fateful year 2304 motorcycles and scooters were built there, after which the industry revived with massive injections of American financial aid. The Meguro was reborn, joined by the Pointer, the Lilac and a modest production called the Honda which was destined for great things indeed. Severe fuel shortage in Japan greatly restricted public transport, and when an imaginative engineer, Soichiro Honda, found 500 tiny war-surplus two-stroke engines he bought them cheaply, and adapted them to run on a substitute fuel based on pine resin. Fitted to ordinary bicycles they sold as fast as his staff of 12 could assemble them in a tiny wooden works in Hamamatsu.

*Cyril Posthumus*

When all 500 engines had been used up, Honda designed his own 50cc unit, and by 1948 his business was organized on a proper footing as the Honda Motor Company. Soon they developed their own pressed steel frames, and by 1950 a Tokyo sales office, and a new factory at Kami-tojo north of the capital had been established, together with a big overdraft. But output of the Honda 'Dream' two-stroke single rose to 300 per month, and with a large government loan the new marque produced a successful 150cc four-stroke model and a new 50cc 'clip-on' two-stroke which they called the 'Cub'. Sales rocketed to over 6000 a month, and the next step was to re-equip the factory with modern plant bought from the United States, Germany and elsewhere.

With his production potential now exceeding domestic demand, Soichiro Honda

**Left: Spain entered the motorcycle industry after the Second World War, and her nimble, sporting two-strokes quickly established an international reputation in trials. This is a 1948 Barcelona-built 125cc Montesa.**
**Below: German postwar motorcycles production was initially restricted to a 250cc top limit; the famous BMW marque therefore reappeared with this neat single-cylinder shaft-drive '250'.**
**Right: Differing vastly from their sleek modern multis is this primitive early Honda, a 1949 Type C with 90cc two-stroke engine and belt drive.**
**Below: A neat Continental, the 1949 500cc Jawa vertical twin from Czechoslovakia had an offset overhead camshaft, unit engine/gearbox construction, and trim lines.**

Honda

Motor Cycle

looked to the United States, Australia and Europe for potential markets, and after weathering another financial crisis the company emerged after 1953 as a new world challenger. The rest of the remarkable 'rags to riches' Honda story belongs to the final chapter, as does the parallel growth of rival Japanese marques such as Suzuki, Yamaha and Kawasaki. Sadly the rise of this vigorous Far Eastern quartet corresponds with the gradual demise of the once proud and predominant British motorcycle industry.

That story, too, is told in the later pages. In the early 1950s, however, the British motorcycle industry still had something to offer the world. The unwelcome 1949–51 period of austerity meant no Motorcycle Show in 1950, even though Britain then was still the world's largest producer of motorcycles, exporting more annually than all other countries put together. About 70 per cent of output still went abroad, many handsome vertical twins suffering aesthetically in the United States by the fitting of 'sit up and beg' or 'steerhorn' handlebars in place of the lower European 'short horns'. The Americans also had a penchant for heavy chrome adornments, while many a bike was 'improved' with brass-studded panniers in cowboy style.

Such flippancies were scorned in Europe, where motorcycles were serious transport, but American sales were far too important to be derided. With cheap petrol and vast mileages to cover, power and comfort were at a premium, and Triumph and BSA answered this in 1950 by producing enlarged twins of 650cc, called the 'Thunderbird' and 'Golden Flash' respectively. Other makers followed suit, Royal Enfield bumping their model up to 700cc as the 'Meteor', while a fast-recovering Germany began muscling in on export battlefields, BMW fielding a new 600cc ohv transverse twin, the R68, destined to grow further into a '750'.

In 1951 petrol rationing at last ended in Britain, stimulating home sales. Total output was some 180 000 motorcycles, but a warning note came in the drop from 70 to 58 per cent in her export figures. In general design changed, but only slowly. The spring frame in its various forms had become so commonplace as to occasion surprise only when absent; wheels tended to become smaller, welded frames were ousting brazing with lugs; the combined saddle and pillion, or 'dual seat' was popular for its convenience and neat appearance; plastics were figuring more widely, being used for fuel and oil piping, cable covering, insulation, screens, etc, while the advent of fibreglass made partial enclosure of mechanical parts a simpler matter.

**Variations on the motorcycle theme.**
**Right: The 1952 Commander was a daring but unsuccessful British lightweight with spine frame made up of square-section tubing, its 197cc Villiers engine caged behind chrome-plated bars.**
**Far right: An early Italian 'superbike', the 500cc MV four-cylinder 'Roadster', based on their famous racing machine and displayed at the 1950 Milan Show.**
**Centre: The AJS 650cc 'Springtwin' typified the British vertical twin of the late 1950s.**
**Far right, bottom: A neat 350cc twin-cylinder two-stroke DKW, the 1953 Model KT.**

### The 'Pipsqueak Show'

But anxiety about living costs sustained British emphasis on lightweights and powered cycles in 1952. So many proprietary engines and conversion units appeared at Earls Court that year that it was dubbed the 'Pipsqueak Show'. Such tiny motors were often of great ingenuity, as instanced by the Tube Investments Company's 'Power Wheel' with rotating 40cc two-stroke engine housed in the wheel hub, and carburettor mounted at one end of the hollow crankshaft. This was one of the last designs by C. G. Pullin, and other British 'eggcup' motors included the Bantamoto, Power-Pak, Minimota, Cymota and Cyklaid, all employing either direct or friction drive. In general these units followed established foreign practice, and the French 48cc Vélo-solex, Italian Cucciolo and Mosquito, and Dutch-built Berini and Mobylette continued to thrive in this ultra-economical class of motorcycling.

A major event in Britain was the re-introduction of branded petrol after 13 years of enduring 'Pool'. When the government introduced it in 1939 the price was 1s 9d per gallon; in its last year, 1952, the price was 4s 7¾d, indicating how steeply prices had risen.

The Ambassador concern, a postwar

RTHPL

**'The Goldie' The 500cc BSA 'Gold Star' was a much-favoured British sports single with fine handling and performance. This is a 1953 model with swinging arm rear suspension.**

Motor Cycle

Motor Cycle

British lightweight marque, announced a luxury 197cc Villiers-powered model with electric self-starting. As it involved two batteries, an extra vee-belt drive, and 20 lb (9kg) extra weight, this praiseworthy effort did not survive long. Triumph digressed from twins with a lively little ohv 150cc 'baby' called the 'Terrier'; its valve gear was similar to that of their bigger engines, but ignition was unusual in embodying a new Wico-Pacy alternator. Ariel celebrated the 21st birthday of their famous aircooled 'Square Four' by giving it a new cylinder head; this had four separate forward-pointing exhaust pipes and the extra power made the famous 'four' a super-luxury 100mph (160km/h) machine.

That a design introduced ten years before the Hitler war broke out should still be in circulation was both creditable yet disturbing; British motorcycle design was indeed stagnating. Exports from Britain had dropped from 91 629 units in 1951 to 70 266 in 1962, indicative of toughening foreign opposition and an end to the sellers' market. Ever-widening industrialization brought ever more manufacturers into the fray. Between 1950 and 1953 alone, there appeared no less than 59 new Italian makes, 42 French, 26 West German, 26 Japanese and 18 Spanish. While many of these were scooters or *vélomoteurs*, they also included the Japanese Honda and Suzuki, the Italian Laverda and Ducati, the Spanish Ossa and Derbi, and the West German Kreidler, all of them strong contenders today. Yet of the seven British makes launched in that same period all but one were short-lived scooters, only the Greeves gaining quick fame as a trials machine and surviving to modern times.

Probably governmental encouragement to produce the maximum number of motorcycles for export had tempted some British makers to utilize their existing factory plant to the full rather than lose production while modernizing. World technology thus unobtrusively overtook them, and the next hint at the malaise that was to assail Britain's fine motorcycle industry and decimate it in the next 15 years came with the 1953 export figures—63 135 compared with just over 70 000 in 1952. Wisdom after the event is all too easy to air; the pressures on the British industry in that time of 'export or die' may seem hard to understand several decades later, but the bitter irony remains that their stupendous efforts to help national survival materially helped to kill many of them off.

# LAST OF THE BRITISH RAJ

"The majority of British machines on show impress by the excellence of workmanship and finish rather than by styling."

*Motor Cycle* editorial comment on the Brussels Show, 1954

It is valid to criticize the long-established British motorcycle industry for failing to introduce more truly new models during the critical 1950s and 1960s. While other European countries were continually announcing exciting modern designs, and Japan was shrewdly feeling her way on to world markets, Britain seemed content to stick with her time-honoured vertical twins and singles. This apathy in allowing foreign competitors to reduce Britain's lead was a major factor in the decline of an industry which had the apparent advantages of top designers and engineers, an unequalled record in advanced motorcycle technology, and the necessary capital, up to a certain stage, to invest in research and development. It is true that design modifications and improvements were continually introduced during this period, but really bold, conceptually new models were few and far between.

Two major reasons for this state of affairs were complacency among the makers, and conservatism among the customers. That very profitability which could have enabled Britain to retain its long-standing lead over the rest of the world encouraged complacency in the boardrooms of the big manufacturers. Time and again promising new designs were shelved or watered down, while the 'bread-winners' of the previous decade were continued, perhaps with a new 'paint job'. With bulging order books and constant encouragement from the government to export as much as possible, there seemed little reason to divert resources into developing and marketing untried new designs. Unfortunately, while such an attitude might get by in a monopoly situation, it was a disaster at a time when more and more imported motorcycles were coming on to the British market.

Moreover, designers with a good memory could partly be excused for their apparent lack of enterprise. In the 1920s and 1930s there had been many attempts to introduce radical new designs, most of which had failed dismally. All too often, excited crowds at the annual Motorcycle Show and favourable press reviews did not lead to orders. To admire a revolutionary design on a stand was one thing, but to spend hard-earned cash on it was quite another, and the average conservative British customer stuck to something sound and sober, if technically dull.

RTHPL

**Above: Phil Vincent caused a storm of interest at the 1954 Earls Court Motorcycle Show with the streamlined 'Black Prince' – a 1000cc vee-twin Rapide with glass fibre enclosure. Vincent himself demonstrates the new rolling centre stand.**
**Opposite, top: At the same show Douglas of Bristol introduced their 350cc 'Dragonfly' with revised suspension system. Swinging arm suspension replaced the old torsion bar system while the 'Radiadraulic' forks were dropped in favour of a Reynolds-Earles pattern.**
**Opposite, bottom: Unfortunately this revolutionary Wooler never passed beyond the prototype stage. Powered by a neat 500cc flat-four engine, with shaft drive and with only two sizes of bolts, the engine unit could be removed in less than 15 minutes.**

Andrew Morland

Popperfoto

Phelon & Moore experienced this when they introduced their 250cc transverse V-twin P & M Panthette in 1927; Matchless with their splendid 600cc four-cylinder 'Silver Hawk' which survived from 1930 to 1935; Douglas with their shaft-drive transverse flat-twin 'Endeavour' of 1936. Such splendid efforts invariably 'stole the Show' but always disappeared from their makers' catalogues in favour of unenterprising, 'safer' designs. It was not the maker's fault, but simply public caution, accentuated by the fact that most members of the motorcycling fraternity were investing a high proportion of their income when buying a new machine, and could not afford to take chances on unproved designs.

The 1954 Earls Court Show echoed the British trend. There were many tidied-up designs, but no bold innovations such as the unit construction of engine and gearbox which was almost a prerequisite on foreign machines. Vincent supplied the one mild shock with their spectacular all-enclosed 'Black Prince', on which the splendid if 'trad' 996cc vee-twin engine was concealed behind plastic shielding enveloping the entire machine from front forks to rear number plate. As soon became evident, this was but a dying kick by a struggling marque. Douglas also drew interest with a new ohv sporting edition of their 348cc transverse flat-twin. Called the 'Dragonfly', it was unusual in having Earles-type front forks of 'leading swinging arm' type, affording ultra-precise steering at the cost of a somewhat clumsy appearance.

### Death of the Vincent

For the rest, it was largely the mixture as before, and the 1955 Show 12 months later gave little more promise. Some ingenious new scooters and mopeds, some enlarged vertical twins, doubtless encouraged by big new British motorway plans, and a tendency towards enclosed driving chains and full-width hubs. Saddest of all was the dying gasp of the proud Vincent marque from Stevenage. Faced with ever-rising production costs on their big 'fire-eating' twins, and seeking wider markets, they first diversified with a useful little moped engine, the 35cc 'Firefly', with friction drive, following this up with a complete motorized bicycle.

In late 1953 they also became British distributors for German NSUs under the name NSU-Vincent. The range included the 'Quickly' moped, the 98 and 123cc ohv 'Fox', the 200cc two-stroke 'Lux', and the 250cc ohc 'Max', with pressed steel backbone frame and unit construction. This venture did not last long; by the close of 1955, when the last few big twins were completed, Vincent

**Right: Most popular moped during the 1950s, the NSU 'Quickly' made no pretensions towards a 'sporty' image but the sturdy little 50cc two-speed two-stroke gave sterling service as a commuter mount.**
**Below: Velocette attempted to appeal to the sporting rider when they introduced the 'Valiant' in 1956. Based on the utilitarian transverse flat-twin 200cc LE, it featured overhead valves, air-cooling and four speeds.**
**Opposite: Royal Enfield introduced the neat little unit construction 250cc ohv 'Crusader' in 1956. This model was developed over the next few years, in an attempt to compete with foreign rivals, and the final version, the GT 'Continental', had a five-speed gearbox and was capable of 90 mph.**

NSU

motorcycle production ended, and the concern turned to other branches of engineering. Another British casualty, only academically mourned since the public of the 1950s never experienced it, was the 500cc flat-four Wooler, a prototype 'dream bike' with alternator ignition, unit construction, shaft drive, and the unusual advantage of standardized nut sizes, enabling the makers to claim the engine could be removed in 15 minutes with just two spanners.

It was around this time that the British road authorities, alarmed at the number of head injuries sustained in motorcycle accidents, began officially to encourage the wearing of crash helmets. There was some call for compulsion even then, but this was felt at the time to be undemocratic, and reliance was placed on common sense to increase the habit of head protection. A component that *was* made compulsory, however, with the spread of television, was a suppressor for motorcycle high tension ignition systems.

Meantime the flow of imported foreign motorcycles steadily increased. Britain's lightweights being, with a few notable exceptions, of uninspired design, it was in the scooter, moped and up to 250cc motorcycle classes that German, Austrian, French, Czech, Dutch, Italian and Spanish manufacturers made their first serious inroads on the British market. The moped class, in particular, was wide open to sophisticated opposition. Formerly known in Britain as the 'autocycle', when 98cc engines were the smallest, they had scarcely developed past the motorized bicycle stage and were strictly for utilitarian transport use. On the Continent, where purchasing and running costs counted even more than in the British Isles, the moped was much more versatile and sophisticated. Many had two or three speeds, spring frames and sporty looks which appealed to the young rider eager to emulate his elders. Emitting sounds like angry wasps, these agile little 'fizzers' started a fashion for sports 50cc models that is still very much around today.

If sales in Britain for these were limited, their staider brethren sold briskly, and even a seasoned lightweight builder like Excelsior

National Motor Museum

decided it was simpler and just as profitable to import the Heinkel moped from Germany as to build their own. Another old British name, Dunelt, reappeared on the tank of a rear-sprung moped powered by a German Rex engine; Norman also marketed an Anglo-German design, and a scrum of other marques disputed an international market in which NSU's practical two-speed backbone-framed 'Quickly' ruled the roost.

### Shortsighted law

Shortsighted British law was largely to blame for the big influx of foreign mopeds. At a 1949 UN conference on road and motor transport, it was agreed by all Continental members that a cycle equipped with an engine of a maximum capacity of 50cc would not be considered as a motor vehicle, and thus would not be liable to road taxation. Only Britain disagreed; moped riders in the United Kingdom would have to pay road tax, wear 'L' plates if unqualified, and pass a riding test. Perhaps the thought of a sizeable proportion of the populace getting away without contributing useful revenue to the state agonized the bureaucrats, but the result was that a potential British moped industry was virtually strangled at birth, and the foreign imports poured in.

The scooters, too, were even more multinational, with the British at least offering some rivalry to the Italian and German favourites. Not all makers tried however, Ambassador importing the Zündapp 'Bella' and Panther the French 'Scooterrot' made by Terrot (though they subsequently produced their own 125cc 'Princess'), while the Stanley concern, former invalid chair makers, took up the marketing of Adler scooters and motorcycles in Britain. Moving up-scale to the 200–250cc motorcycle class, several British makers contested the foreign invasion, and in 1956 world affairs provided an unexpected incentive. The Suez Canal crisis boiled up, the price of petrol rose to 6 shillings a gallon, and rationing was introduced in Britain for a short period just before the Motorcycle Show.

Interest suddenly focused on lightweights, mopeds and scooters, and demand showed an encouraging rise. A new class of clientele, the motorist unable to face the increased cost of driving to work, or frustrated by the stop-and-start rush-hour traffic, was taking up motorcycling on a purely utility basis. One result was a strengthening in the 250cc class, which was augmented by an attractive new unit construction ohv Royal Enfield with fully enclosed rear chain, the 'Crusader', while AMC of Woolwich decided to make their own 250cc two-stroke single-cylinder engine/gear unit for the group's Francis-Barnett and James models instead of buying Villiers engines. The latter concern, celebrating the completion of their two millionth proprietary engine in 44 years, continued untroubled with an output of 5000 units per day and full order books.

A further development in the lightweight class was a new sporting Velocette, the 192cc 'Valiant', which was basically of flat-twin shaft-drive LE derivation, but with aircooling, pushrod ohv, and foot-change for the four-speed in-built gearbox. And down in the scooter 'basement' BSA produced a new 70cc model, the 'Dandy', which came midway between a moped and a scooter, and was an interesting exercise in modern steel presswork with its curved backbone frame. The engine was installed to one side of the rear wheel, Vespa-wise but with the cylinder to the rear, and forming part of the swinging rear fork; preselector two-speed transmission was another feature, but the machine's ugly appearance was against it.

### Italy takes over in racing

The decline of British motorcycling influence in the 1950s never showed more plainly than in international racing. Her famous single-cylinder ohc Nortons, Velocettes and AJSs were now totally eclipsed by the Italian Gilera, MV and Guzzi multi-cylindered bikes. Nor was there any comfort in the smaller categories, for tiny watch-like Italian MVs, Guzzis and Mondials dominated the 125 and 250cc classes, while sidecar racing was solidly German territory, ruled by BMW. In the six classics constituting the 1956 World Motorcycle Championship, no single event fell to a British motorcycle, a shattering reversal after so many years of domination. It was thus a much-needed boost for Britain when an American, Johnny Allen, broke the world motorcycle maximum speed record with an ultra-streamlined 650cc Triumph 'Thunderbird' engined projectile at a speed of 214.4mph (345km/h) on the Bonneville salt flats in Utah. Yet even this feat turned sour when the international authorities delayed recognition of the American figure.

There was no 1957 Motorcycle Show. The industry decided to follow Continental practice and make it a biannual event. Modern

*Motor Cycle*

**Right: The big surprise of 1958 was the new Ariel 'Leader' powered by an inclined 250cc two-stroke unit-construction engine with coil ignition and enclosed drive.**
**Left: To appeal to the conservative British market, the 'Leader' was offered in a 'naked' version as the 'Arrow'. The tuned 'Arrow Super Sports' (pictured here) was capable of over 80 mph (130 km/h).**
**Below: Norton joined the 250cc market with the twin cylinder ohv 'Jubilee' which appeared in 1958.**
**Bottom: One of the classic sports singles, the 500cc high-camshaft Velocette Venom 'Clubman' Mark II offered impressive performance combined with dependable handling. It was still in production as late as 1971.**

*National Motor Museum*

long-term tooling for 'continuity' programmes and forward-planning made the 12-monthly show both a burden and a bore, with little change in models set up for a long production run. The wisdom of this was manifest at the next show, in 1958, when sufficient novelties justified the two years' wait. Obviously British makers had made some effort to combat the overseas challenge with some enterprising new models. Outstanding was the Ariel 'Leader', representing a drastic break with tradition by the famous Birmingham marque which by then had become a member of the BSA group.

Its designer was Val Page, who started the cult for the vertical twin with his 650cc Triumph of 1933, and the magazine *Motor Cycle* was moved to comment that "seldom since the earliest days of motor-cycling can a new model have embodied quite so much novelty as does the 249cc Ariel 'Leader' . . . Great credit is due to the Ariel directors for having the enterprise to present it." The design featured a pressed steel, box-girder type frame giving full enclosure, pressed steel trailing link front forks, an inclined twin-cylinder two-stroke engine with horizontal cooling fins, unit engine/gear-box construction, coil ignition, fully-enclosed rear chain and a distinctly attractive finish. Externally its rakish lines dated most contemporaries, but at first the makers hedged their bets and continued to market their classic 'thumper' singles and the perennial 1000cc 'Square Four'.

The 250cc class brought other newcomers, one, surprisingly, from Norton, whose 'Jubilee Twin' was a colourful miniature of their larger vertical twins with stylish rear fairing and enclosed rear chain. AMC launched virtually identical Matchless and AJS unit construction ohv 250cc singles of very clean design, and BSA also contributed a new 250cc ohv single, the 'Star'. In other capacities there was a bewildering selection recalling pre-war days: BSA with singles up to 600cc, not

*Motor Cycle*

forgetting the trusty old side-valve M21 almost unchanged from the 500cc M20 of the war years, and vertical twins; Norton still with their big pushrod ohv singles and the 'Dominator' twins featuring the 'Featherbed' frame and 'Roadholder' forks that continued to set the standard for handling for years to come.

AMC's vast range, encompassing James, Francis-Barnett, AJS and Matchless, covered everything from small two-strokes to 650cc twins; Triumph and Royal Enfield had their twins and lightweights too, while Velocettes ranged from the LE and 'Valiant' small twins to their 350 and 500cc high-cam 'Viper' and 'Venom' singles – fine sturdy performers though basically pre-war designs warmed up with alloy cylinders and rear springing. Depressing was the demise the previous year both of the Sunbeam and Douglas twins, but that other brave 'independent', Panther, was still in the running, surprising all in producing a 'super-plonker' by enlarging their historic 'Sloper' single to a record 650cc to lure side-car enthusiasts, while still making smaller two-strokes, four-strokes and scooters.

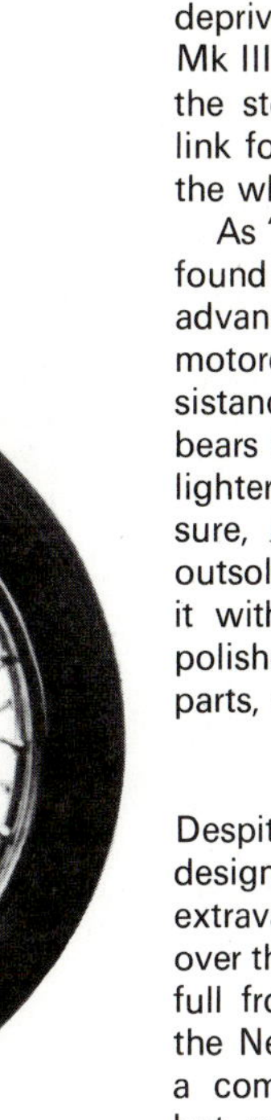

Withal it was a brave showing, but not brave enough to combat cold commercial calculation. Helped by cheaper labour, more up-to-date designs and modern production facilities, the foreign infiltration increased as the 1960s came in. In 1959 Ariel had taken the plunge and concentrated production on the 250cc twin two-stroke 'Leader'. This deprived the discerning motorcyclist of a Mk III Ariel 'Square Four' which had been on the stocks, and was to have Earles leading link forks and the most regal specification of the whole long line of Ariel fours.

As 'Leader' production rose, however, Ariel found – like Sunbeam before them with their advanced twin – that the average British motorcyclist of 1960 showed that same resistance to the unusual that his 1930 forebears had done. They therefore introduced a lighter, cheaper version minus the full enclosure, calling it the 'Arrow'. It immediately outsold the 'Leader', so they supplemented it with the 'Arrow Super Sports', giving it polished engine externals and other brighter parts, and a racy-looking screen.

### Enclosure for some

Despite this rebuff to cleaner motorcycle design, other makers were indulging in an extravaganza of parts enclosure, especially over the rear wheel. Royal Enfield also offered full frontal protection, while Velocette aped the New Hudson and Triumph of 1932 with a combined crankcase and gearbox cover, but using moulded plastic instead of sheet metal. As a make with a great racing pedigree, moreover, they hit on a most effective demonstration, both of their bike's stamina and the effectiveness of its streamlining. A 500cc high-camshaft 'Venom Clubman Vee-line' was taken to the Montlhéry high speed track near Paris in March 1961 with a team of seven British and French riders to attack long-distance records. In one weekend Velocette became the first motorcycle in the world to travel at over 100mph (160.93km/h) for 24 hours. Their actual average was 100.5mph (161km/h) and they also took five interim world records in a highly convincing performance.

That the 'Venom's basic design originated in the Velocette MSS of 1934 did not escape some critics, but a far more remarkable survival was the Scott, the watercooled parallel twin two-stroke power unit of which dated back to 1908! Ultra-enthusiasts for this smooth, tractable and still impressively accelerative motorcycle brought it through a 1950 bankruptcy and re-established the company in Birmingham. Swinging arm rear suspension, and a four-speed gearbox were the main improvements, and the 600cc 'Flying Squirrel' was sold in strictly limited numbers to discerning customers, the makers requiring assurance that buyers were worthy of their

Motor Cycle

Andrew Morland

**Far left: The bike that shattered European complacency – the 1962 305cc parallel twin Honda 'Dream'. Faster and more comfortable than many established 500s, its specification included indicators and an electric starter, considered luxuries at the time. Opposite, below: Mainstay of Norton's reputation during the 1950s and 1960s, the 'Dominator' series started with this 500cc version, but was later developed into the 600cc model '99' and the 650cc 'Super Sports', capable of over 115 mph (185 km/h) and the forerunner of the later 750cc 'Atlas'. Left: A fantastic lesson in longevity, the twin cylinder two-stroke watercooled Scott was first built in 1908, and is still available to order today, 70 years later.**

machine before accepting an order! Such dedication to an historic design poses a typically British enigma to hard-headed Continentals seeking only to produce the best modern design to the best commercial advantage, but the motorcycle world would be infinitely poorer without such apparently eccentric survivals.

On the import-and-export front, however, there was no sentiment, and a British industry which was beginning to lose its way was losing the battle. The number of foreign machines landed on British quays increased monthly, and the scooters, mopeds and 'nopeds' (50cc bikes minus the pedals) were supplemented by bigger-engined 'babies' of 100, 125, 150 and 200cc. Bianchi's 'Falco 50' first came to Britain in 1959, followed by the 75cc 'Gardena', the 125cc ohv 'Bernina' and the 175cc 'Tonale'. With four speeds and a neat unit-construction ohv engine this latter machine was an eye-opener in a country served with 175s such as the three-speed two-stroke BSA 'Bantam', based on a prewar design.

Another Italian make, Capriolo, followed the same pattern, introducing their 75cc 75TV at the same time as the 'Falco', then importing 100 and 125cc models, all featuring four speeds and ohc engines. More Italian makes followed, notably Ducati and Moto-Guzzi. Both employed lightweight ohv or ohc engines in advanced frames, and both, significantly, were pathfinders for bigger capacity multi-cylinder models destined in the 1970s to attack the once impregnable bastion of the home industry.

## Strong opposition

The 'Buyers' guide' in a mid-1961 issue of a motorcycling magazine gives a striking picture of the situation. European machines then marketed in Britain included Adler, Atala, Bianchi, BMW, Bultaco (a highly promising new Spanish lightweight), Capriolo, Ducati, Gilera, Guzzi, Itom, Jawa, MV, NSU, Puch and Zündapp. Adding scooters and mopeds to the list, further names include Capri, Diana, Heinkel, HMW, Iso, Lambretta, Maico, Motobécane, Mobylette, Prima (NSU), Prior, Rumi, TWN, Vélosolex, Vespa and Bella (Zündapp). Some 30 years earlier efforts to import just one German make, the Zündapp under an English name, had aroused wide interest!

It must also be remembered that most of these continental makes were being exported to dozens of other countries in direct contention with British machines. While the United States, for example, took large quantities of Britain's bigger vertical twins in the 1950s, a considerable number of German machines of all sizes and prices were also sold there for precious dollars. Among the makes which found a market there were BMW, Maico, NSU, Victoria, Hoffmann, TWN, Horex, DKW and Zündapp, and these were followed in the 1960s by the Italians and, of course, the Japanese.

In 1961 only one foreign motorcycle import into the United Kingdom was Japanese. It bore the name Honda, which had then already given lie to the old charge that the Japanese were only good at copying other designs, and that since a copied article was invariably inferior to the original, there was nothing to worry about. Japan's invasion of Europe had begun two years earlier, spearheaded by the Honda 'Dream', an apt name considering its specification. This included a

**Right: Out like a lamb . . . Final two-wheeler product of the once proud Ariel marque, former makers of prestigious sporting singles and luxury four-cylinder models, was the little 50cc 'Pixie' moped of 1963. This and the subsequent three-wheeled 'Three' moped sounded the death knell of a famous British motorcycle. Bottom: Big Briton. Royal Enfield's 700cc 'Meteor' vertical twin, shown in its 1953 form, served well as a punchy solo or an indefatigable sidecar mount.**

*Motor Cycle*

247cc high-compression ohc parallel twin engine with electric starting, fully enclosed chains, and the refinement of 'winker' direction indicators.

A beam-type frame in which the engine served as a down-tube, Panther-style, was used, and the pressed-steel leading-link front forks looked heavier than they were. Moreover, this dynamo-smooth 250 was faster and better-braked than several British 350cc singles costing about the same, but with the added luxury of infallible electric starting. Indian of the United States had tried this feature in 1914, Ambassador of Britain in 1952, and doubtless a few hopefuls in between, but Honda were the first to make it *work* and render the kickstarter obsolete at last.

As it had so often before in motorcycle history, racing contributed vitally to the evolution of the Honda. After a quiet but thorough 'recce' of the Isle of Man TT scene in 1958, the Japanese entered a team of five tiny ohc parallel twins in the 125cc Ultra-Lightweight race in 1959. They couldn't match the fierce pace of the race-matured Italian MVs and Ducatis, or the East German MZs, but four of the Hondas finished sixth, seventh, eighth and eleventh, and won the team prize – a considerable feat on their first appearance. They went home to digest what they had learned. Three years later the fabulous multi-cylinder Honda machines won the 125, 250 and 350cc World Championships, taking first place in every one of the 25 races they contested! Japan had arrived in world motorcycling with a vengeance.

### Unity is strength?

With pressure increasing all round, British manufacturers resorted to that long-established expedient of closing their ranks and grouping together, investing their faith and their capital in the belief that 'Unity is strength'. Logically it made economic good sense to reduce the number of independent models; there were half a dozen British vertical twins, all variations on a common theme, in com-

*Lewis & Sons Ltd*

*Motor Cycle*

**Right: Last of the line. The 650cc vertical twin Matchless 'Monarch' of 1967 was the final model before the sad demise of a famous marque founded in 1899.**
**Below: The name 'Spitfire', used on an illustrious fighter aircraft and subsequently on a British sports car, was also applied to the BSA 650cc twin in the 1966 two-carburettor Mark 2 Special sporting form.**

*National Motor Museum*

petition with each other, and numerous sporting singles and lightweights too. This was democratic free trade, but in the contracting markets of the early 1960s some of it looked like wasted effort. Yet a study of the fortunes of the major British manufacturing groups that were formed indicates that here, too, things went awry.

The fates of Norton, Triumph, BSA, New Hudson, Matchless, AJS, Villiers, James, Francis-Barnett, Sunbeam and Ariel were all decided by one such grouping; each had a long and fascinating history, but now a new and, for some, sad chapter of their story was to unfold. AJS became linked with Matchless in 1931 when the former ran into financial trouble, and under the name Associated Motor-Cycles (AMC) the two makes became increasingly similar until, by the mid-1950s, they were virtually identical. The first outside company to be absorbed by AMC was Sunbeam, but the purchase, made in 1936, proved to be a mistake, and the famous company then passed under the wing of the fast-growing BSA group of companies early in the Second World War. As has been recorded, the last Sunbeam motorcycles were the advanced S7 and S8 in-line twins, production of which ceased in 1958, after which the once-revered name appeared only on a scooter.

James and Francis-Barnett, both prominent makers of two-stroke lightweights, were the next 'independents' to become part of AMC. They quickly lost their individuality and within a few seasons the only differing feature was the colour scheme – red for a James, green for a Francis-Barnett. The last James roadster, the 250cc 'Sports Superswift' powered by a Villiers 4T two-stroke engine, was dropped in 1966, while a 250cc trials model disappeared a month later. Francis-Barnett had a wider range, encompassing single and twin-cylinder two-strokes between 150 and 250cc, with 250cc trials and scrambles variants which performed well in those exacting spheres. Nevertheless, the name disappeared at the same time as James.

The other marque to join the AMC camp was one of the most famous of all – Norton. The merger was effected in 1953, the companies continuing as separate entities until contracting markets made rationalization of production necessary. In 1963 Norton production was moved entirely from the famous Bracebridge Street factory in Birmingham to the AMC plant in Plumstead Road, Woolwich. By 1965 'Norton' motorcycles were emerging with lamentable evidence of cross-breeding, using Norton engines in Matchless frames, and sometimes vice versa. The only lightweight was the 250cc 'Jubilee' twin, while the 350cc Model 50 Mk II was virtually a Matchless G3 with Norton badges on the tank. The 'Navigator' 350 and 'Electra' 400 ohv twins remained real Nortons, but the type ES in Mk II form was simply a Matchless G80 with Norton nameplates.

### Enter Norton-Villiers

In 1966 things came to a head. Deep in debt, the AMC group was wound up and Manganese Bronze Holdings Ltd, a company headed by Dennis Poore, took over the business. MBH had themselves taken over the Villiers engine manufacturing business some months earlier, and the new combine was called Norton-Villiers Ltd. There was a note of optimism in an early news bulletin issued by the new proprietors: "Production is again in full swing at the AMC factory following the acquisition by Villiers . . . Five famous marques have been saved from extinction by a deal between the AMC receiver and Manganese Bronze Holdings, of which Villiers are a subsidiary. All five marques, AJS, Matchless, Francis-Barnett, James and Norton are being continued, and the Woolwich factory will remain in operation for at least a year."

Despite these comforting words both James and Francis-Barnett perished only a few months after the takeover. The last Matchless 250, the 'Monitor 90', was dropped

**Right: While older British makes fell one by one, the Essex-built Greeves motorcycle, founded in 1952, has forged into international prominence with a mounting list of successes in trials, scrambles and racing. Shown here is the 1954 197cc twin cylinder two-stroke 'Fleetwing' road model, its rider in typical 1950s gear.**
**Far right: European arm for the American Harley-Davidson concern until the mid-1970s was the Italian-built Aermacchi, a small, brisk performer of advanced concept. This 175cc four-stroke horizontal model is the 'Ala Rossa' sporting roadster.**

Motor Cycle

that same year, the 650cc 'Monarch' vertical twin went within another couple of months, and the last machine to bear the once proud Matchless tank badge, the 750cc G15 CSR, was dropped the following year. All former AJS models were also dropped, the make re-emerging a year or so later as a potent 250cc two-stroke trials and scrambling machine. All Norton single-cylinder models were dropped, but the 650 and 750cc vertical twins were continued.

Thus, by drastic rationalization, did Norton-Villiers bring their motorcycle production within reasonable bounds. The story of their progress into the 1970s, the decade of the 'super-bike', and their subsequent struggle to survive will be discussed later, but meanwhile other British marques had also been learning the pros and cons of grouping.

For many years the BSA motorcycle branch of the great Birmingham Small Arms organization had been one of the largest and most diversified of British makes. During the Second World War they acquired both Sunbeam and New Hudson, the latter a long-established Birmingham-based firm which gave up motorcycle manufacture in 1933; five years later, however, they began producing 98cc autocycles which sold well during the austere war and early post-war years. In 1947 the BSA empire expanded further when they took control of Ariel of Selly Oak, Birmingham, one of the oldest of the 'independents'. Four years later another major British marque passed under their wing when they acquired the Triumph company for over £2½ million, BSA emerging as easily the largest motorcycle manufacturers in Western Europe.

In the 'golden '50s' there was little need to rationalize production, and the parent company wisely left the Ariel and Triumph model ranges alone, all three building their own vertical twins. An Edward Turner-designed 150cc 'Terrier' ohv single was added to the Triumph range in 1954, enlarged a year later to 200cc and renamed the 'Tiger Cub'. Following the introduction of the advanced 250cc twin two-stroke Ariel 'Leader', however, production of all other Ariels – singles, vertical twins and the famous 'Square Four', was dropped.

Unlike AMC of Woolwich, the BSA combine had the advantage of many other engineering interests within their organization to provide capital support. In 1961, their centenary year, they had acquired the Churchill Machine Tool Co. which, with other connections, made them the largest machine tool concern in Britain. They were so diversified, in fact, that no less than 30 separate companies operated within the group in over 20 main factories, producing a wide variety of goods from coal cleaning plant to taxicabs – and motorcycles.

### A Sunbeam scooter

They were thus spared the fate suffered by AMC, and advanced into the 1960s under the banners of three world-renowned motorcycle makes. To try and cash in on the scooter boom they also introduced the so-called Sunbeam scooter in 1959. Powered by a 250cc vertical twin four-stroke unit construction engine, this was bigger, heavier and more luxurious than the Italian models which started the craze in Britain. In 1963 it was equipped with 12-volt lighting and an electric self-starter, but this Sunbeam was not a success and was dropped a year later.

Triumph, too, had been persuaded to dabble in the scooter pool, and their automatic transmission 100cc 'Tina' and 175cc 'Tigress' were both more successful than the Sunbeam, being lighter and more Italian in styling. A 250cc 'Tigress' was simply the Sunbeam under another name and was equally short-lived.

National Motor Museum

BSA's own range was extensive, comprising the well-known 'Bantam' lightweight which had grown through the years from 125 to 150cc, and then to 175cc, and had a good reputation as a relatively crude but economical and sound 'bread-and-butter' bike; a unit-construction ohv '250' which performed well in sports, trials and scrambles versions; unit construction 350 and 441cc ohv singles, and the range leaders, the A50 and A65 vertical twins to a variety of specifications. Production of the much-loved B34 Clubman 'Gold Star' high-performance 500cc ohv single was dropped in 1963, to general regret, as was the last pre-unit construction 650cc twin, the A10 'Road Rocket'.

The climax to the BSA group story is tied in with that of Norton-Villiers, but it should be recorded at this stage that a few independent British firms still operated, notably Velocette and Panther. Some smaller firms such as Dot, Cotton, Greeves and Rickman vigorously supported off-road activities such as trials and scrambling, making lively two-stroke lightweights. Dot and Rickman offered 'do it yourself' machines in kit form, which in spheres where cash was tight but engineering ability high, proved very popular.

### The big Harleys

As the profusion of British and other European motorcycles crossed the Atlantic to the all-important dollar markets, American motorcyclists grew replete, and enjoyed the luxury of becoming 'choosy', so that competition between importing makes intensified. Incredibly amid all this, the one surviving domestic American marque, Harley-Davidson of Milwaukee, still found a market for their big, heavy, old-fashioned vee-twin roadsters. By the early 1960s two modernized models had arrived, both of which were to make a lasting impression: the 1000cc pushrod ohv 'Sportster' which was fast, with a very sporty image; and the 1200cc Electra-Glide which made a big impression in all senses.

It had been standard equipment with American police departments for years, and was designed as a long-distance tourer. The soft springing and luxury fittings on this great thumping 'two-lunger' appealed to many American riders, while its innate strength made it a favourite with the class of motorcyclist seeking sheer dependability without having to dirty himself tinkering.

A shrewd board of directors at Milwaukee realized, however, that the company could not operate profitably on the sales of dated big twins and three-wheeled commercial adaptations of same. The Italian Aermacchi concern of Varese, producers of lively lightweight machines, became available for take-over in 1958, and Harley-Davidsons became the new proprietors. While wisely retaining a separate European-based directorate, and continuing a racing programme which has brought great international prestige to Harley-Davidson, this European link widened the American company's influence considerably.

With the British motorcycle industry heading irrevocably for the twilight, one further contributory cause merits mention. In Britain motorcycling had for many years been regarded as a sport in which a little extra noise, the odd spot of oil, the need to tinker to gain efficient running, and to dress as for an Arctic expedition, were all treated as 'part of the game'. Utility lightweights were used by commuters, but the 'men's machines were designed with a sporting, 'cobby' look, feel and sound about them.

With enthusiasts, this complex endured even into the 1960s, when the big British singles still seemed to be holding their own against the foreigners. But dirt, discomfort and noise were no longer acceptable; the scooter with its in-built leg and facial protection was an eye-opener; the de luxe lightweight with windscreen, silent motor and all comforts, such as the LE Velocette or the Guzzi 'Galletto' was another. Such machines, which did not leak oil but were quiet, unobtrusive and efficient, attracted a new class of motorcyclist who would never have considered riding the traditional 'rorty' type of machine.

The Japanese makers showed a clear appreciation of these factors by designing rather than adapting their machines to be comfortable, trouble-free, and as easy to operate as possible, whereas too large a proportion of the British industry, accustomed for years to cater for the self-sufficient type of rider, could not so easily adjust. By recognizing market trends and acting quickly, the opposition gained the vital 'edge' that made the 1966–76 decade such a disappointing one for Britain.

# THE JAPANESE AGE

"I regard the sales potential for Honda two-wheelers in Europe as limitless."
Soichiro Honda at the opening of the first European Honda plant in Belgium, 1963

The first infiltration of Japanese motorcycles on overseas markets came in the lightweight classes. This was both logical, since these were their *forte* at home, and sensible, since world demand for cheap and frugal transport was ever increasing as civilization spread. Their early conquests left the long-established European makers untroubled, and British firms in particular fondly imagined that the Nipponese challengers would confine their attention to the low-capacity brackets, leaving the well-proven British vertical twins to continue ruling the 'big bike' roost. They had a shock coming.

The origins of Japan's 'big four' manufacturers show remarkable variation. As related in earlier pages, Honda was founded in 1948 by a shrewd engineer who was also an opportunist, who found some surplus two-stroke engines, adapted them to bicycles, and launched a giant new concern. Suzuki was a much older company, founded in 1909 by Michio Suzuki for the production of textile machinery, but which switched to motorcycles in 1952 when a major recession threatened their staple line. Yamaha, whose first motorcycle came along in 1954, had earlier links going right back to 1887 as makers of pianos, organs and other musical instruments, which explains their interesting 'crossed tuning forks' trade mark.

As for Kawasaki, veterans who served in the Far East during the Second World War will need little reminding of the name. This industrial giant was founded back in 1878, building ships, locomotives, rolling stock, heavy machinery, submarines and aircraft before setting up a branch to join in the motorcycle boom. The first model bearing their name was a 50cc moped launched in 1961, but their involvement in the trade went further back, Kawasaki 60cc two-stroke and 125cc ohv motorcycle engines having been made since 1949 under the name Meihatsu. In 1961 Meihatsu was reorganized as the Kawasaki Auto Sales Company, which arranged a deal with a small independent factory, Meguro, whereby the latter's 500cc ohv vertical twin, a virtual copy of the BSA A7 'Shooting Star', was distributed through Kawasaki outlets only, alongside their own proprietary engines.

To gain recognition in a Japanese market dominated by the ever-rising Honda, Kawasaki aimed for a sporting image. In 1963 their B8M motocross model, evolved from a standard 125cc roadster, took the first six places in the Japanese motocross championship. By 1965 they had opened their first American sales office in Chicago, offering a range of two-strokes from 90 to 250cc which combined commendable agility with reliability. American sales rose, and soon Kawasaki were exporting over 90 per cent of their production. To cater for the American liking for powerful, sporty twins, they then introduced the Meguro – but with Kawasaki badges on the tank and a 650cc engine fitted.

With its pre-unit construction and right-hand gearchange this still looked remarkably like a BSA. This most British of all Japanese export models was short-lived, however, for in 1969 Kawasaki took over the Meguro company completely, dropped the dated twin, and introduced a whole new range of potent three-cylinder two-strokes to spearhead an assault on European markets.

## The Honda miracle

Needless to say, Kawasaki's compatriot rivals had also been working hard to develop their export ranges, none more efficiently than Honda. Following the success of their 250cc parallel twin 'Dream' in Europe, they introduced a brilliant 50cc two-stroke machine, the 'Super Cub', which captured world-wide popularity in the vast utilitarian markets at the expense of scooters and mopeds. A measure of its success lies in the production figures: over 24 000 in 1958, the year of its introduction, over 167 000 in 1959, and up to 800 000 by 1962! These were feats of precision mass production unheard of at British factories in earlier times, and that same year Honda were well established as the world's largest producers of motorcycles in the world's largest motorcycle factory (just one of three they operated in Japan) at Suzuka.

One reason for this success, which would have seemed totally unbelievable ten years earlier, was that the clean, practical design of Honda road machines, their ease of control, comfort and general appeal, did not simply draw sales away from rival machines – they actually *made* vast new markets amid a public disenchanted with the cost and inconvenience of motoring and seeking an extra new mode of personal 'pleasure' transport to supplement the essential motorcar. The American public were especially receptive to this, as indicated by Honda sales there; these exceeded 5000 machines per month by 1962, and between 1957 and 1963 comprised over one-third of all Honda's formidable exports.

With their totally commercial, not to say ruthless, policy of winning markets, Honda could well afford to employ 400 full-time research staff, commanding an annual budget of over £700 000, to keep their products and production methods up-to-the-minute. It all paid off, as did their devastating assault on

Yamaha

Opposite: Staple product of the flourishing Honda marque, the 50cc 'Cub', with two-speed gearbox and automatic clutch, has been sold in huge numbers all over the world to people needing reliable, basic transport for one. This is the 'Sport' version.
Left: The first Yamaha, the model YA1, powered by a simple little 150cc two-stroke engine, and looking like a cross between the BSA Bantam and a German DKW. Unusually for a Japanese bike, the rear suspension features plunger springing.
Below: Mr Soichiro Honda himself rides the ten millionth Honda motorcycle to be built off the production line in 1968. Such an output is unsurpassed in the motorcycle world.

Motor Cycle

Motor Cycle

**Left: Austria has attained new prominence in world motorcycle sport with the rise of KTM, which initials derive from the manufacturers, Kronreif & Trunkenpolz, and Mattighofen, the site of their factory. KTM won the 1977 250cc World Motocross Championship.**
**Below: One of Japan's 'big four', Suzuki made their name with excellent lightweights and racing successes before building larger models, such as this GT500 two-stroke twin of 1976-77, a popular model developed from the T500 'Cobra' which appeared in 1968, making the series the longest running from any Japanese manufacturer.**

international racing, which cost them very large sums of money but gained invaluable prestige. Their fantastic 125cc racing twins and 250cc fours, with four valves per cylinder, twin overhead camshafts and six-speed gearboxes, just swamped all opposition in 1961 and 1962. As is the way of racing, their success drew new opposition, much of it from rival Japanese marques, but meantime Honda were inevitably looking at the over 250cc markets beyond their own shores.

The appearance of a new 350cc class road model, the 305cc CB77 with an ohc two-cylinder engine, 12-volt lighting and electric starter, deliberately coincided with a new Honda onslaught on the 350cc (Junior) racing class in 1962. With this fierce four-cylinder machine they won five 350cc classic races in 1962, six in 1963, and eight in 1964. By 1966 they moved higher yet, into the 500cc (Senior) class, and again new racing successes coincided with the launch of a new road bike. This was the twin ohc CB450, a model which by its high performance and colour scheme gained the nickname 'Black Bomber', while basking in the limelight of sensational new Honda wins in the 500cc racing class, spearheaded by Senior TT triumphs two years running, in 1966 and 1967.

### In Honda's footsteps

In striving to keep up with Honda's runaway pace on the European and American markets, two other major Japanese makers, Suzuki and Yamaha, backed up their production programmes with some intensive racing activity. In 1953, their first full production year, Suzuki had built over 4400 two-stroke lightweights, and they rapidly increased this to six-figure outputs in subsequent years. Nine years later, in 1962, still specializing in high-speed two-stroke power units, they won the first-ever 50cc T T race in the Isle of Man, and in the 1963 125cc TT Suzukis took the first three places. They also won eight European classics, defeating the rival Hondas each time, and capitalized on this to offer their roadsters on the British market that same year. The Suzuki range of 50, 80 and 250cc two-stroke models swiftly became a major force on Western markets.

Again following in Honda's footsteps Suzuki then developed a bigger machine to challenge the Western '500's. Their T500 'Cobra' twin-cylinder two-stroke reached Europe by 1968 and soon gained acceptance as a tough, reliable touring motorcycle. With the tuning equipment that was available 'over the counter' it also scored notably as a clubman's racer, and today, ten years later, a modified version still features in the Suzuki range.

When the first Yamahas reached Europe in the early 1960s, their range of two-strokes from 55 to 250cc were, in common with other Japanese makes, very advanced in comparison with their European counterparts. Indeed, the little 55cc Yamaha MJ2 even sported a 12-volt electric starter – something unheard of on any comparable Western design! Then, following the same road that Honda and Suzuki so successfully took, Yamaha plunged into the hurly-burly of international road racing, scoring their first TT win in the 125cc class in 1965, backed up by no less than seven 250cc wins in Germany, France, Spain, Holland, the United States, Czechoslovakia and Finland. By 1969 their five-speed 350cc YR3 roadster was competing successfully with many Western 500s and soon Yamaha, too, were up in the 'big bike' league.

### The writing on the wall

With such a bewildering variety and volume of superior Japanese machines pouring on to the European markets, the British motorcycle industry's trade balance suffered seriously, and rising import figures competed with falling exports in sombre significance. In 1966, British mopeds and scooters were still failing to drive off foreign rivals, while just over 30 000 motorcycles, mostly lightweights and mostly Japanese, had been imported. Offsetting this, 58 900 British motorcycles had been exported, most of these being vertical twins. Triumph's 650cc 'Bonneville' and BSA's similar A65 remained attractive sporty machines, popular in North America which was far and away Britain's biggest export market. Of over £14 million worth of British machines, spares and accessories exported during 1966, BSA and Triumph accounted for over 80 per cent, and both companies won

Motor Cycle

**Above: Desirable 'Duke' – Italy's 90° vee-twin Ducati, shown here in its 1971 750cc form, is a potent roadster, readily adaptable to production racing. Below: Despite the modern trend towards bigger and bigger engines, the 500 remains immensely popular. This is Honda's very popular CB500.**

New Motorcycling Monthly

the Queen's Award to Industry in 1967–68. Considering the conditions and the ever-mounting opposition, these last plaudits were probably deserved.

### Italy fights back

Japan was not the only country to turn its attention to larger motorcycles. The Italians, declining to fall into the same trap as Britain of resting on their laurels, and uncomfortably aware of the Japanese 'big four's global offensive, took a long, hard look at the situation. Scooters had long been their most lucrative export, but the boom of the early 1960s was ending. British sales, for example, had dropped from 20 900 in 1966 to only 8700 by 1969, and there were similar drops elsewhere. So Italian designers, too, went higher up the capacity scale.

Ing. Giulio Carcano, a designer of near genius who had masterminded Moto-Guzzi's very successful postwar racing programme, had produced a neat 750cc ohv transverse vee-twin with shaft drive for the Italian army and police in 1965. A lighter, sleeker version was developed for civilian use, giving 42 bhp and a maximum speed of 106mph (170km/h). Although riders in few countries could ever fully exploit such speed, the 'magic ton' had tremendous appeal with the sporting young men who formed so important a proportion of the world's motorcyclists. Moreover, a machine with such potential is obviously unstressed when performing at lower speeds. The 'over 100mph' cachet helped to make the transverse vee Guzzi an immediate success as a high speed touring model, particularly in the United States where vee-twin orientated riders found the Italian bike vastly superior to their home-brewed Harley-Davidsons.

**Right: Similar in overall style to the Ducati, the 350cc ohc vee-twin Morini also has typical 'racy' styling which has helped to make it one of the most successful Italian medium weights. Below: Italian 'Superbike', the 750cc parallel twin Laverda GTL of 1974–75 could top 125 mph (200 km/h), and figured prominently in production racing. The latest disc-braked Laverda twins and threes have a considerably higher performance.**

Another Italian marque, Ducati, also graduated to larger machines, offering a 350cc edition of their popular 250cc ohc 'Monza' in 1966, following up with the 450cc 'Desmodromic' single, and then moving firmly into the high-performance market with a 90° ohc vee-twin 750cc model by 1971. Its engine was installed lengthwise, with the forward cylinder disposed horizontally and the rear just ahead of the saddle, and this reversion to the allegedly dated vee-twin layout was echoed on a smaller Italian machine, the 350cc Morini.

Then the Laverda, a make founded in 1949 when they built scooters, boldly abandoned lightweight production altogether, concentrating instead on an exceptionally fast ohc parallel twin, first as a '650' in 1968, and then as the SF750, which quickly established itself as one of the most exciting, if expensive, production machines on the market. Workmanship and finish were superb, and Laverda soon showed their capabilities by some fine performances in long-distance production motorcycle racing.

With such machines was born the modern 'Superbike' class, and the old and honoured German firm of BMW, faced with a double threat in this class from Japan and Italy, had to 'pull their socks up' too. Production of their famed if costly ohv 'Boxer' twins had dropped from 25 000 bikes in 1952 to only 6000 per year in the late 1960s. By 1969 production at the Munich works was right down to 4700, and there were possibilities that BMW would drop its motorcycle interests completely. With its proud pedigree and technical prowess at stake, however, a big effort was made, capital invested in new plant and equipment, and a modernized range was developed. Featuring 12-volt lighting and electric starting on the two larger models, the three-bike range of 500, 600 and 750cc shaft-driven flat-twins proved an immediate success, and by 1971 sales were back up to 20 000 a year. This was good news for the Germans, but just one more problem for the ailing British motorcycle industry, depleted early in the new decade by two more famous makes which went under – Royal Enfield and Velocette.

### Great names die

The Royal Enfield demise was unusually complex. By 1968 their only model still in production was the 750cc vertical twin 'Interceptor'. In an effort to ease financial problems

**Right: Although Royal Enfield dropped the 350cc 'Bullet' in 1962, the model, as well as the marque itself, are kept alive today in the Madras-built Enfield-India. Still featuring a pre-unit gearbox, and 1950s styling, the Enfield is not only successful in India, but is even being imported into Britain. Below: The highly impressive Kawasaki 498cc two-stroke triple 'Mach III' of 1969 earned a dubious reputation for its exceptional performance, offset by inconsistent handling.**

*Motor Cycle*

the factory was moved from Redditch to Bradford-on-Avon, in a wartime underground plant formerly used to house art treasures from the National Gallery. A new 800cc version of the 'Interceptor' was on the drawing board, but it was too late, the Enfield concern folding in June 1970 after a 70-year career in the motorcycle industry.

The name was not to die out completely, however. Manganese Bronze, 'parents' of the modern Norton-Villiers group, maintained its investment in an Enfield-India subsidiary based in Madras. There 350cc 'Bullets' and a 173cc 'Crusader' two-stroke continue to be made today at the rate of about 25 000 annually, chiefly for the Indian army, police and civil service, and for African markets. In a fantastic turn-round of events, these Indian Enfields are now being exported to Britain, and were exhibited at the 1977 Earls Court Motorcycle Show.

The death of the classic Velocette was particularly sad. In the late 1960s their punchy high-camshaft ohv 500cc singles could still be sold in a British market saturated by smooth twins. The 200cc LE Velocette, still modern underneath with its BMW-style transverse flat-twin engine and shaft drive though dated externally, also remained in production thanks to contracts with various police forces. However, the company had made a great mistake in trying to cash in on the scooter market with their elaborate 'Viceroy' model introduced at the tail end of the boom. It was beautifully engineered, but too large and expensive to appeal to riders attracted by the neatness, simplicity and cheapness of the Vespa and Lambretta, and sales were poor.

Having borrowed £75 000 to tool up for 'Viceroy' production, the Veloce company found itself with outstanding debts of £92 000 and went into voluntary liquidation in June 1970. An attempt to continue as a general engineering concern was unsuccessful, but motorcycle production dragged on at a rate of two or three per week until February 1971, when Veloce Ltd was finally closed down after 68 years of distinguished existence. There was hope for a time that E. & H. P. Smith, who already controlled Alpha Bearings and Albion, the gearbox makers, might take over Velocette and keep production going. Talks broke down, however, and the famous Velocette works at Hall Green, Birmingham, were sold off.

### Company convulsions

While Royal Enfield and Velocette were in their dying throes, the two major conglomerates, AMC and BSA-Triumph, which by now virtually controlled the whole British motorcycle industry, were each undergoing further convulsions. Associated Motor Cycles (AMC) had been taken over by Villiers, a subsidiary of the Manganese Bronze group, in 1965. The AMC name was dropped, and the company rechristened 'Norton-Matchless Ltd'. By 1967, however, the name was changed again, to 'Norton-Villiers', following the demise of the Matchless marque.

As recounted in the previous chapter, Dennis Poore, chief executive of Manganese Bronze, had to adopt a very hard-headed attitude towards the new company if it was to survive, and production of all member-makes apart from Norton was dropped to avoid duplication of effort. To manufacture the new updated range of Norton twins, Manganese Bronze spent a cool million pounds on a new factory at Andover, Hants, to replace the famous old AMC works in Plumstead, which were closed for good in 1971.

Production of Villiers proprietary two-stroke engines at Wolverhampton was also stopped, a sensible move if the company was to concentrate on 'heavyweights', but a devastating blow to small independent British makers who relied on Villiers motors for their lightweight trials and scrambles machines. Greeves were able to survive by making their own engines, but Dot and Sprite were among those which disappeared, marking yet another downward step for the fast-contracting British industry.

It also added to import figures, of course, since foreign engine makers took advantage

Motor Cycle

**Left: Last of a great line, the AJS marque survives today in the 250cc two-stroke 'Stormer' motocross machine built in Andover. While no world beater, the 'Stormer' is still a reasonably competitive model. Right: British 'three'. The 1970 750cc BSA 'Rocket III' seemed to have all the requisites of success with its fine performance and appearance, but the BSA Group decided to rationalize the BSA and Triumph ranges, and the model was short-lived. Below, right: Japanese 'four'. The 750cc Honda CB750 – the ultimate sports tourer for thousands of modern enthusiasts. Undoubtedly the most successful of all the Japanese heavyweights, set the standard for all Japanese transverse fours.**

of the situation. Sachs of Germany began supplying two-stroke units to small British companies including Rickman, who had for a time produced a sporting roadster using Enfield 'Interceptor' engines. British mopeds, such as the AJW, were also to appear in the 1970s using imported engines, mostly of Italian Minorelli or Morini make. The designs, tools and prototypes from the Villiers works were transferred to a newly formed 'AJS Division' of Norton-Villiers, where 250cc and 410cc 'Stormer' motocross two-stroke models were developed to help the group maintain some sporting interests. Both models were offered in kit form and then as complete machines in 1973, but were soon dropped when further company structural changes were made.

Meantime Norton, one of the most prestigious names in motorcycling, carried the main N-V banner with a condensed range of vertical twins. The 'Dominator' series had come a long way from the original 500cc model 7 of the 1950s. Their 'Roadholder' forks and 'Featherbed' frame earned them a well-deserved reputation for handling, while the engines grew to 600 and then to 650cc capacity. The last 650cc 'Dominator Sports Special' had twin carburettors and an over-115mph (185km/h) maximum.

In 1963 AMC had introduced a successful 750cc version of the 'Dominator', called the 'Atlas', for the American market. It sold less well in Britain, possibly because British riders did not have the American obsession with size and were content with a well-proven '650'. In 1968 Norton-Villiers replaced it with the 750cc 'Commando', a model destined to become a mainstay of the industry as well as the last large-capacity machine to appear under the Norton name. Using the same 73×89mm bore and stroke as the 'Atlas', the 'Commando' engine was inclined and mounted in an entirely new frame featuring the revolutionary 'Isolastic' principle wherein the engine, separate gearbox and pivot bearings for the swinging arm suspension were all carried in a sub-frame, rubber-mounted within the main duplex frame, securing a high degree of frame rigidity with the minimum of vibration.

The 'Commando' was an immediate success in Britain and overseas, earning £1 400 000 in American exports in the 19 months up to July 1970, and £1 600 000 in Australasia in the same period. Having dropped the last 650cc model, the 'Mercury' in 1970, Norton-Villiers put all their hopes into the 'Commando' to maintain their hold in the heavyweight market in the 1970s.

### BSA-Triumph ups and downs

The BSA-Triumph group entered the last period of its history on the crest of a wave, contributing a large proportion of the 56 200 British machines exported in 1970. The former lassitude had gone, and the industry seemed to be fighting back at last. Unfortunately, some serious errors of judgment were made by the group's management, that were to do great harm within a short time. In February 1967 a new research and development division was established at Umberslade Hall, and while the staff there produced some worthwhile designs, it was at cost of £750 000 added to the group's annual overheads.

Another error attended the release in the autumn of 1968 of the most exciting new British motorcycle for years – the three-cylinder Triumph 'Trident'. This had an advanced 750cc in-line engine set across the frame; bore and stroke and many components were of Triumph 500cc twin origin, which was sensible design rationalization, and the acceleration and 115 mph-plus maximum (185km/h) speed were impressive. A BSA 'Rocket III' version, virtually identical apart from having an inclined instead of vertical cylinder block, was introduced at the same time to attract confirmed BSA enthusiasts

**Norton's last model, the vertical twin 'Commando' lasted until 1977. This is the 'Hi-rider' version, built for the American market. The 'Commando's natural cobby appearance is marred by the high-rise 'apehanger' handlebars and the clumsy seat, incorporating a pillion backrest.**

Motor Cycle

and keep BSA dealers happy, but Jack Sangster, a veteran of the industry, warned that 'badge engineering' or duplication of models of this kind would not only raise distribution costs but would adversely affect pride of ownership, as had happened with the identical BSA 'Sunbeam' and Triumph 'Tigress' scooters.

The new 58bhp 'triples' were a 'last ditch' effort by BSA-Triumph to resist foreign competition in the 'Superbike' class, and their debut was unfortunately followed a few months later by a new 67 bhp Honda four-cylinder 750cc road bike with five-speed gearbox, huge disc front brake and electric starter, plus a maximum speed exceeding 120mph (192km/h). The new BMWs came out at around the same time, as did a new machine from Benelli of Italy, the 643cc vertical twin 'Tornado'. There were also rumours of a 750cc watercooled Suzuki 'three' which in fact materialized in 1971, so that competition for BSA-Triumph's new venture was formidable, to say the least.

Motor Cycle

Despite this they did well initially, American sales being boosted by some success in production racing. The Japanese story had reminded BSA-Triumph that good racing performances helped sales, and 'Tridents' ran second and third in the prestigious Daytona 200 Miles race in 1970, while the following year a 'Rocket III' won outright, followed by a 'Trident' and another 'Rocket III'. A 'Trident' also won the 1970 Production T T race in the Isle of Man, a feat repeated in 1971 at an average of over 100mph (160km/h) with two more of the British 'triples' following home. 'Tridents', indeed, dominated the production T T for the next five years, in view of which it was unfortunate that the BSA group management should commit another blunder.

Under the misconception that there was a worldwide demand for a three-wheeled 'shoppers' lightweight, much money and effort was invested in developing a 50cc two-stroke Ariel moped called the 'Three'. Some expensive publicity followed, but the machine,

Right: A classic American marque, the Indian lives on in lightweight two-stroke trial bikes such as this ME100 Enduro model, designed and marketed in California, but built in Taiwan, using many Italian components.
Below: Proving its stamina, Percy Tait winning the 1974 Production TT on a 750cc Triumph Trident 'triple' – the Triumph's fourth win in four years. Despite this, NVT stopped production of the Trident early in 1977.
Below, right: The very antithesis of traditional Harley-Davidson design is this 90cc lightweight two-stroke, designed to appeal to the huge American 'fun bike' market.

Motor Cycle

Motor Cycle

the last to bear the proud name of Ariel, failed completely. In the critical few weeks after its introduction in 1970 only a few hundred were sold, and despite price-cutting from £110 to £88 by 1972 in an effort to dispose of them, the BSA group lost over £2 million as a result of this fiasco.

A further mistake was the old one of trying to produce too many models. In 1971 no less than 13 new or modified models were offered by the group, upsetting production, distribution, delivery and hence sales. The most interesting of these new models was a 350cc twin ohc Triumph 'Fury', with its inevitable 'identical twin', the BSA 'Bandit'. Aimed at contesting the Japanese mediumweight range, they were prematurely publicized and a huge investment in tooling up was lost when major faults were discovered, only a few prototypes being completed.

Such mismanagement hastened the group's demise. Profits had fallen sharply in 1969 and 1970, while 1971 showed a catastrophic deficit of £8 500 000. The usual measures were taken; the model range was rationalized *à la* Norton-Villiers, BSA's last vertical twin 500, the 'Royal Star', and the 250 and 440cc 'Gold Star' and 'Victor' singles all being dropped. It could not stop a further £3 300 000 loss in the 1972 financial year, and with bankruptcy threatening, talks were arranged between the Department of Trade and Industry, the BSA group, Manganese Bronze Holdings and Norton-Villiers.

As a result, the two groups, Norton-Villiers and BSA-Triumph, were combined into one company – a company which, with the Norton 'Commando' and Triumph 'Trident' as well as the BSA and Triumph twins, should be able, it was felt, to compete on more equal terms with the foreign challenge. In July 1973 the great BSA group ceased to exist as independent manufacturers, and the new organization, comprising virtually the whole of the British motorcycle industry, was formed. It was called Norton Villiers Triumph, or NVT.

### A Kawasaki '900'

Meantime the foreign 'superbikes' multiplied. Kawasaki, following reorganization in 1969, had augmented their range with a 500cc three-cylinder two-stroke, the 'Mach III', possessing considerable performance. It was also relatively cheap, though built to exacting

**Latest and greatest from Kawasaki is the KZ1000, with 1000cc transverse four twin ohc engine developing 82 bhp at 8000 rpm with a top speed of almost 125 mph (200 km/h). The Kawasaki 'fours' have justly become legends in their lifetime.**

Motor Cycle

standards with the most modern technology, but weight distribution and handling limitations gave it a 'sudden death' reputation. In 1972 it was replaced by a new four-stroke ohc 'four', set Honda-style across the frame, and with the formidable capacity of 900cc. Its performance and refinement were such that it was voted 'Bike of the Year' both by *Motor Cycle* and *Motor Cycle News* in Britain, although its primary target was obviously the United States.

Yamaha introduced a large machine in 1972, breaking their two-strokes only tradition with a zestful 650cc ohc twin. America's defence against this combined onslaught rested solely with Harley-Davidson and their big twins, since a welcome revival of the Indian make in 1969 was in the under-200cc

**Right: From East Germany, the Schopau-built MZ is one of Europe's toughest and most reliable two-strokes with a proud racing history, and a fine reputation in 'enduro' events. This is the 1977 TS150 model.**
**Below: From Russia with love . . . the BMW origin of the rugged 650cc Cossack shaft-drive flat-twin is particularly evident in this sidecar version. The Cossacks sell at highly competitive prices on the European markets.**

*Motor Cycle*

*Motor Cycle*

class, with 'enduro' and trail bikes actually built in Taiwan though designed in the United States. Harley-Davidson's impressive 1200cc ohv 'Electra-Glide' (now also offered as a 1340cc model) still led their range, but the 1000cc 'Sportster' was evolved to compete with the foreign products, backed up by the 1200cc FX, having the same pre-unit construction engine as the 'Electra-Glide' but with 'Sportster' styling.

While Japanese, Italian, German, British, American and other nations' motorcycles thus competed for the world's custom, it need not be surprising that Soviet Russia, too, dipped into this great commercial turmoil. With major factories at Minsk, Kiev, Izhevsk and elsewhere, she sought sales outlets beyond Eastern Europe, and the Russian strong point was not high performance or 'superbike' quality, but cheapness and dependability which could appeal to the commuter markets in Germany and other West European countries, and even North America. The Cossack 'Dnieper' and 'Ural' models are 650cc near-replicas of the old ohv shaft-drive flat-twin German BMW; the 'Jupiter' is a 350cc two-stroke twin, while there are also Planeta, Voskhod and Minsk single-cylinder two-strokes, some with quite sporting pretensions but all providing sound, inexpensive transport.

An interesting feature of Russian motorcycles, shared by the East German MZ and Czechoslovakian Jawa, is that they are available in combination form with matching sidecars. This practice died in Britain with the P & M Panther, but indicates a returning popularity of sidecar outfits in recent years. The well-known British make, Watsonian, continued sidecar production throughout the 1960s when other manufacturers pulled out due to lack of demand, and now other firms like Squires and Siderider are producing new ranges of sidecars in modern materials. Not surprisingly, single-seat sidecars suitable to the modern breed of 'superbike' are predominant, but recently small makers have even turned out double-adult sidecars which present a strange sight when coupled to a modern multi-cylinder roadster!

**Left: British tiddler, the only NVT model still in production, the 'Easy-Rider' moped is powered by an Italian Morini engine and is offered in a variety of specifications, this being the 'sporty' model.**
**Below: The 'Bonnie'. Produced by the Meriden cooperative, the 750cc vertical-twin Triumph Bonneville is truly the last of the British Raj in the motorcycling world. This 1977 model is one of the limited edition built to mark Queen Elizabeth's Silver Jubilee.**
**Bottom: 'The power unit of the future' was how many authorities described the Wankel rotary engine. This is the neat 1976 NVT prototype. The rotary engine has yet to gain wide acceptance from the motorcycling public.**

## The NVT situation

Despite that hopeful start, the modern British motorcycle industry, as represented by Norton Villiers Triumph has not fulfilled its early promise. The Triumph manufacturing plant at Meriden, outside Coventry, was closed by NVT after being plagued by industrial disputes. After a long, drawn-out struggle lasting 18 months the factory reopened as a government-sponsored workers' cooperative, and is still manufacturing 750cc Triumph 'Bonnevilles', but for NVT itself the future is uncertain.

All production of BSA twins was stopped in 1971; of the BSA 'Rocket III' in 1972; and of 650cc Triumph twins in 1975. Concentrating on the Triumph 'Trident' and Norton 'Commando', which was enlarged to 830cc in 1973, NVT declared a deficit of £3 600 000 for the 12 months up to July 1974, putting them £5 784 000 'in the red' overall. The 300 'Commandos' produced every week at the Wolverhampton factory, along with 200 'Tridents' from the old BSA works at Small Heath, were selling well but in an attempt to recapture at least a small part of the moped market NVT introduced their 'Easy Rider' range, powered by Morini engines imported from Italy. These have now been joined by Italian powered 125cc and 175cc 'Rambler' trail bikes, but unfortunately the NVT range has not made much impact on a market dominated by Italy and Japan.

Other ventures by this hapless organization which came to nought include the creation of racing machines to regain their former prestige, and development of a Wankel-engined motorcycle. Production of the 'Commando' and 'Trident' has now come to a halt. The impact of these disasters is seen in recent British export and import statistics.

In 1973 a reasonable 49 600 motorcycles were exported, most of them 'Tridents', 'Bonnevilles' and 'Commandos'. In 1974 the number fell to 23 200, in 1975 to 21 500, and in 1976 to 14 800 – this from what was once the greatest motorcycle-producing country in the world. With the demise of the 'Trident' and 'Commando', the 1977 figure will be even lower. At the same time motorcycle imports rose from a total of 194 960 in 1973 to a staggering 309 100 in 1976; of these, only 2200 were scooters, 78 300 were mopeds, and 228 600 were motorcycles.

## Intriguing variety

The current situation, then, shows the once proud and sometimes haughty British motorcycle well down, if not entirely out, while the foreign makers enjoy the fruits of far-sightedness, up-to-the-minute production plants and methods, and freedom from the combined political, economic and labour problems which have so afflicted Britain in recent years. The design variety on offer to the modern motorcyclist is fascinating. The transverse four-cylinder motif, pioneered by Gilera on their racing machines before the Second

Motor Cycle

Motor Cycle

Left: As Italian as Chianti, finished in bright Italian red, the 1974 Moto-Guzzi 750cc 'Sport' looks every inch the thoroughbred that it is.
Right: Portugal first entered the world's motorcycle market with the Casal range of two-strokes, built in Aveiro, some 36 miles south of Oporto. This K270 is a 125cc single-cylinder model.

Motor Cycle

Opposite, below: The German Hercules, powered by a 249cc single-rotor Wankel engine, was the first rotary engined motorcycle to go into production. Marketed in Britain under the DKW banner, the ultra-modern looks of the Hercules match its up-to-the-minute concept.

Below: A 'Ferrari' of the motorcycling world – the high price of the MV-Agusta 750S 'America' is offset by its four-cylinder dohc engine, double-disc front brake, five-speed gearbox, shaft drive and 136 mph (220 km/h) top speed.

Motor Cycle

**Right: Bespoke Briton. Descended from the classic twin-cylinder two-stroke Scott, this custom-made machine, the 'Silk', hails from Derby. Powered by a 653cc all-aluminium watercooled twin-cylinder engine with transistorized ignition, the latest model 700 SPR costs £2050 – and there's a long waiting list of eager customers!**
**Below: Powered by a beefy transverse 'triple' engine of 980cc, the Laverda '1000 Jota' is capable of a shattering 140 mph (225 km/h) which is matched by a close ratio five-speed gearbox, double disc front brake, transistorized ignition and high-quality finish. At the time of writing, the 'Jota' is the world's fastest production motorcycle.**

*Motor Cycle*

World War, rates the most popular today, employed by various manufacturers, including Honda, Kawasaki, Suzuki and Yamaha of Japan, and by Benelli and MV of Italy.

Honda also introduced the impressive hyper-luxury 'Gold Wing' with 1000cc water-cooled flat-four engine in 1975, with a revised version planned for late 1979, Kawasaki and Suzuki have enlarged their 'fours' to the full 1000cc. Yamaha have gone up to an 1100cc 'four' while Honda have gone right up to the mighty six-cylinder 1000cc CBX. The search for more power, though sometimes seeming ludicrous considering modern road conditions, continues apace. Laverda's latest offering, the 1000cc 1977 Paris Show they showed a 1200cc version. Since then Kawasaki have topped this with their latest 'megabike', an awesome watercooled 1300cc transverse six.

Moto-Guzzi still build their transverse vee-twins, including a 1000cc version having automatic transmission – a significant trend – while the Ducati vee-twin has grown to 900cc and Benelli offer intriguing variety with 750cc and 900cc sixes and a range of lightweights. MV-Agusta produce the 750S 'America' with 800cc transverse four-cylinder engine, shaft drive and an impressive purchase price of over $6000, while the latest 'Boxer' is at present the world's fastest production machine at over 141mph (227km/h)! BMW of Germany are not far behind in price with their latest 1000cc transverse flat-twin.

The Wankel rotary engine, with its lure of simplicity, few reciprocating parts, compactness, silence and flexibility, has inevitably attracted some technical adventurers. Yamaha introduced a watercooled 497cc five-speed Wankel-powered machine at the 1972 Tokyo Show, but have now dropped it; Suzuki also dabbled in rotary power plants with their short-lived RE5; a Sachs-built 294cc rotary engine is used in the German DKW Hercules, while the Dutch 996cc Van Veen prototype employs a Comotor development of the Wankel. So far no real breakthrough has been made by this type of power unit, which is notably 'dirty' in an emission-conscious mechanical world, and may yet prove a costly 'white elephant'.

Two exotic, highly potent machines. Below: The 1000cc Honda 'Gold Wing' with its flat-four watercooled engine, shaft drive and luxury equipment. Bottom: The Benelli 'Sei' is the only machine to feature a transverse six-cylinder ohc 748cc engine. Capable of around 125 mph (200 km/h), the 'Sei' is one of the more unusual models in the Italian 'superbike' range.

Honda

Benelli

**Right: True to the company's proud racing tradition, the modern Italian Gilera range features a variety of very clean-lined two-stroke lightweights, offered in touring, sports and off-road specifications, exemplified here by the 150cc single-cylinder model T61. The Gilera marque has been owned by the Piaggio group (makers of Vespa scooters) since 1969.**
**Below: In an era dominated by multi-cylindered models, Yamaha sprang a surprise in 1977 with their XT500 'Enduro' ohc single-cylinder trail bike which features a device almost unheard of today – a valve lifter to ease kick starting! There is nothing old-fashioned about the bike's performance however, its top speed approaching 100 mph (160 km/h).**

*Yamaha*

As to the smaller-engined classes, to list all the modern contenders would turn this work into a catalogue. Suffice it to record that well over 50 different makes from at least 18 different countries – Britain, France, West Germany, Austria, East Germany, Czechoslovakia, Poland, Soviet Russia, Sweden, the Netherlands, Switzerland, Italy, Belgium, Spain, Portugal, the United States, India and Japan – were building and selling motorcycles in 1978. And out of such incredible cosmopolitan variety, Britain still merits a brief footnote – for if the British industry is dead, it stubbornly refuses to lie down!

Matt Holder, whose Aerco company retains the rights to the names of Royal Enfield, Velocette and Scott, still produces a small number of 600cc Scott 'Flying Squirrels' to special order, while Silk Engineering of Derby offer a custom-built 680cc watercooled twin based on Scott design – and there is a two years' waiting list for one. Remarkably, Ariel

**Right: The Spanish Ossa company is famous for its lightweight trials machines, but it also produces this 500cc two-stroke roadster, a high-performance sports machine, virtually a doubled-up 250 racer.**
**Opposite, top: Arguably the best touring machine of all, and undoubtedly the most sophisticated – the 1977 BMW R100/RS. Powered by a 1000cc flat-twin ohv engine, the biggest BMW can be cruised comfortably at well over 100 mph (160 km/h), while the fairing is designed to keep the rider happy at any speed.**
**Far right: France is less active in the modern motorcycle industry than might be expected. This is the three-cylinder 350cc two-stroke Motobécane, built by a combine claiming to be the world's largest manufacturers of mopeds and bicycles.**

BMW

Motor Cycle News

'Square Fours' are also available to order from Healeys of Redditch, who build a modernized version of the Mk II with 12-volt lighting and direction indicators.

Two motocross machines of great potential are the CCM, with modified BSA B50 engines of 500, 580 and 600cc, and the Bolton-built EMC which uses Sachs two-stroke engines. Perhaps most exciting of all are the prospects of a new 1000cc vee-twin Weslake engine being developed at a small factory in Rye, Sussex. Having produced a world-beating 500cc ohc speedway engine, a doubled-up Weslake '1000' is a mouth-watering prospect. There is also a possibility of a five speed unit construction 90 degree vee twin roadster.

In the course of its long and chequered history, the motorcycle has changed from a novelty to a fast, efficient means of transport and pleasure. It has taken many forms, and even now appeals to different types of rider in different ways. Specialist models have been developed for road racing, trials, motocross, sand racing, speedway, grass-track, sprinting and, of course, road riding in all its forms. We have seen how the present day breed of machines evolved, but what they in turn will develop into can only be conjecture. Of one thing we can be certain: the motorcycle story is still unfolding, and if past events are any guide to the future, it will not be boring.

# INDEX



Picture reference in italics